New Seafood Cookbook

The Confident Cooking Promise of Success

Welcome to the world of Confident Cooking,
where recipes are double-tested by our team
of home economists to achieve a high standard
of success—and delicious results every time.

bay books

C O N T E

Barbecued tuna and Mediterranean vegetables, page 67

Won ton wrapped prawns, page 23

Salad niçoise with seared tuna, page 53

Sashimi timbales, page 37

N T S

Easy seafood paella, page 78

Lobster mornay, page 101

The Publisher thanks the following for their assistance: Bertoli Olive Oil; Breville Holdings Pty Ltd; Chief Australia; MEC-Kambrook Pty Ltd; Sheldon & Hammond; Southcorp Appliances

Fish and chips, page 83

Scallops with pasta, page 46

All recipes are double-tested by our team of home economists. When we test our recipes, we rate them for ease of preparation. The following cookery ratings are on the recipes in this book, making them easy to use and understand.

A single Cooking with Confidence symbol indicates a recipe that is simple and generally quick to make—perfect for beginners.

Two symbols indicate the need for just a little more care and a little more time.

Three symbols indicate special dishes that need more investment in time, care and patience—but the results are worth it.

IMPORTANT
Those who might be at risk from the effects of salmonella food poisoning (the elderly, pregnant women, young children and those suffering from immune deficiency diseases) should consult their doctor with any concerns about eating raw eggs.

Succulent Seafood

With the wonderful array of seafoods available, we have no excuse for not having an excellent diet.
Most seafood has a low fat content as well as valuable vitamins, minerals, protein and fatty acids.
All types of seafood should melt in your mouth so here are a few tips to help you attain that goal.

Seafood has unfairly earned the tag 'difficult to cook', partly because in some cases it can require varying amounts of preparation for cooking. The perception of seafood cookery being daunting has persisted in spite of the fact that seafood cooks relatively quickly. Although the methods of cooking are the same as for meat, fish, for example, doesn't have as much connective tissue as meat, so it breaks down more quickly when heat is applied.

To add further weight to the 'difficult' tag, many species of seafood, especially fish, have ended up with more than one common name, often leading to confusion. We try to address some of these problems by providing you with a chart at the back of the book showing alternative names of various species. Obviously, it is not possible to list every species, so we have tried to choose the most commonly available.

Within our recipes, we have explained how to prepare your seafood before cooking, although you may prefer to ask your fishmonger to do it for you. Usually, he will be happy to do so.

We hope to inspire you to experiment with different types of seafood and where possible, we have listed alternatives if the first choice of fish or other seafood is not available.

TYPES OF FISH

The most common descriptions of seafood are firm, soft, oily and dry.

Most fish have a relatively firm flesh that holds together during cooking. Fish with soft flesh require more gentle cooking methods such as poaching and steaming.

Oily fish have the fat content dispersed throughout the flesh. Most white fish have drier flesh because they store fat in their livers.

If fish have a lighter-coloured flesh, this often indicates a more delicate flavour. Freshwater fish usually have a sweet taste, although some have a strong and sometimes slightly muddy flavour.

PREPARING YOUR FISH

To scale fish, scrape against the direction of the scales with a spoon or fish scaler.

Slit the fish belly, then remove the gut. Rinse under cold water, then pat dry.

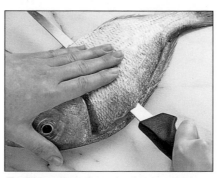

To fillet, slice close to the bone along either side of the body.

CHOOSING SEAFOOD

We all know that seafood should be absolutely fresh when we buy it. But if it doesn't actually smell 'off', can we tell just how fresh it is?

Seafood is divided into three main categories (fish, crustaceans and molluscs) and each category has particular characteristics that we can look at as a good indication of the freshness.

WHOLE FISH:
● Eyes should be clear, bright and bulging (avoid fish that have dull, sunken and cloudy eyes)
● Skin and flesh should have a lustrous appearance and feel firm. If a fish can easily be bent so its mouth can kiss its tail, it is probably past its prime
● Fish tails should be moist and pliable, not dried out
● Fish with scales should have a good even coverage and if patchy-looking are best avoided. Scales should be firm and intact
● Gills should be bright (from bright to dark red, depending on species).

FISH FILLETS/CUTLETS:
● Fillets or cutlets should look moist and lustrous and have no signs of discolouration. The fish on display should not be sitting in liquid
● Fresh fish fillets should not look dried at the edges.

CRUSTACEANS (prawns/shrimp, crabs, lobsters, bugs, freshwater crayfish):
● No discolouration or 'blackness', particularly at the joints (claws, nippers, heads etc.)
● Bodies, claws, nippers etc. should be fully intact, not broken or missing
● Bodies should be free of water or liquid and should be heavy in relation to size.

LIVE CRUSTACEANS (usually blue, black or green):
● Should be active and moving freely. Nippers and claws should be intact, not broken or loose
● Mud crabs should be tied up until after they have been killed.

All crustaceans should feel heavy for their size. Crustaceans shed their shells as they grow and, after about 4 months, they grow into a new shell. If they feel light, it may mean they are still growing and, if so, the flesh will be watery.

MOLLUSCS (invertebrates with soft unsegmented bodies and often a shell):
univalve (one shell) e.g. winkles, whelks, abalone;
bivalve (two shells) e.g. mussels, oysters, scallops:
● Shells should be tightly closed, or close quickly after a tap on the bench, be intact and look lustrous. Flesh should be firm and 'plump';
cephalopods (octopus, cuttlefish, squid):
● Flesh should be firm and resilient and spring back when touched
● Head, tentacles and body should be intact and not loose.

REFRIGERATING

FISH FILLETS/CUTLETS:
Prepare whole fish by scaling, gutting and cleaning, then rinsing under cold water. Pat dry to remove any traces of scales or intestinal lining (or ask your fishmonger to prepare the fish). Place in a covered container (or in a freezer bag on a plate) in the coldest part of the fridge and use within 2–3 days.

CRUSTACEANS AND MOLLUSCS:
Wrap large crustaceans such as crayfish, lobsters and crabs in foil, then place in a container or on a plate.

All other shellfish can be placed in a covered container or in a freezer bag on a plate. Store in the coldest part of the fridge and use within 2–3 days.

Use raw crustaceans and molluscs (prawns/shrimp, crabs, lobsters, oysters) within 1–2 days of purchase.

To keep mussels, pipis and freshwater crayfish alive, store in a bucket of cold water in the coldest part of the house. Cover the bucket loosely with a damp cloth and keep away from direct sunlight. They can be kept in the refrigerator in hot weather for up to 3 days.

FREEZING

Ideally, all seafood is best eaten fresh. However, you can freeze it when it is very fresh.

When buying fish, make sure it hasn't already been frozen. Label and date for freezing. Don't defrost frozen seafood at room temperature: thaw in the fridge. Some seafood, such as crumbed fish fillets, calamari or prawns (shrimp), can be cooked from frozen. Avoid refreezing seafood as this alters the flavour and texture.

Whole fish, fillets and cutlets: Scale, clean and gut, rinse under cold water, pat dry with paper towels, then freeze in an airtight bag. Whole fish can be frozen for up to 6 months (oily fish such as tuna, mullet, Atlantic salmon and sardines, can be frozen for up to 3 months). Fillets and cutlets should be frozen in bags in smaller portions for up to 3 months.

Prawns (shrimp): Do not peel. Place in a plastic container and cover with water—this forms a large ice block which insulates the prawns (shrimp) and prevents freezer burn. Freeze for up to 3 months. When required, thaw in the refrigerator overnight.

Other crustaceans and molluscs: Freeze for up to 3 months. Wrap large crustaceans such as crayfish, lobsters and crabs in foil, then place in an airtight freezer bag for freezing. Octopus, squid and cuttlefish should be gutted and can be frozen for up to 3 months. Oysters shouldn't be frozen as the flavour will alter.

COOKING SEAFOOD

As you will discover when using the recipes in this book, seafood is very versatile. It lends itself to steaming, poaching, baking, barbecuing and grilling (broiling), stewing and casseroling, stir-frying, deep or shallow frying, as well as marinating or coating. Seafood should never be overcooked or it will be dry, tough or rubbery. It should be removed from the heat as soon as it is 'just done'—the internal heat will finish the cooking process.

But how can we tell when the moment is right? Most seafood is cooked when it loses its translucent appearance and turns opaque. Fish starts to flake apart and separate from the bone. Some seafood, such as tuna and Atlantic salmon, is best served while it is still rare in the centre.

Fish fillets are used extensively in cookery because of their versatility. Cook them as soon as possible after purchase so they don't dry out.

Molluscs can be cooked briefly or eaten raw. The shells can be prised open—you may need to cut the muscle, or they can be steamed open. As with most seafood, don't overcook molluscs or the flesh will toughen.

Small octopus can be barbecued, grilled (broiled) or fried, but larger ones need to be tenderized by the fishmonger, then need long simmering in liquid. When tenderized, the tentacles curl up.

Small cuttlefish and squid are delicious fried and the bodies are ideal for stuffing. Large cuttlefish and squid require long simmering.

SERVING YOUR FISH

Run a spoon or knife down the centre of the fish, then pull the fish from the bone.

Lift out all the bones and cut off near the tail. Serve the flesh in sections.

SOUPS

BOUILLABAISSE

Preparation time: 40 minutes
Total cooking time: 30 minutes
Serves 6–8

Rouille
1 small red capsicum (pepper)
1 long red chilli
1 slice white bread, crusts removed
2 cloves garlic
1 egg yolk
80 ml (1/3 cup) olive oil

300 g (101/2 oz) raw medium
    prawns (shrimp)
18–24 black mussels
200 g (7 oz) scallops
1.5 kg (3 lb 5 oz) assorted white
    fish fillets
2 tablespoons oil
1 fennel bulb, thinly sliced
1 onion, chopped
5 ripe tomatoes, peeled, chopped
1.25 litres (5 cups) fish stock
pinch of saffron threads
1 bouquet garni
5 cm (2 inch) strip orange rind
chopped parsley, to garnish

1 For the rouille, cut the capsicum and chilli into large pieces and discard the seeds and membrane. Grill (broil) skin-side up until the skins blacken and blister. Cool in a plastic bag, then peel. Soak the bread in 60 ml (1/4 cup) water, then squeeze out excess liquid. Combine the capsicum, chilli, bread, garlic and yolk in a food processor. With the motor running, add the oil in a stream, until the mixture is smooth.

2 Peel the prawns and pull out the dark vein from each back, starting at the head. Scrub the mussels and pull out the beards. Discard any broken mussels, or open ones that don't close when tapped. Slice or pull off any vein, membrane or hard white muscle from each scallop, leaving any roe attached. Cut the fish into 2 cm (3/4 inch) pieces. Cover and refrigerate the seafood.

3 Heat the oil in a large saucepan over medium heat and cook the fennel and onion for 10 minutes, or until golden. Add the tomato and cook for 3 minutes. Stir in the stock, saffron, bouquet garni and rind. Bring to the boil and cook for 10 minutes. Reduce the heat, add the fish, prawns and mussels and simmer for 4–5 minutes, or until the mussels open (discard any unopened ones). Add the scallops and cook for 1 minute. Remove the bouquet garni and orange rind. Ladle the bouillabaisse into bowls, garnish and serve with the rouille.

NUTRITION PER SERVE (8)
Protein 58 g; Fat 23 g; Carbohydrate 7.5 g; Dietary Fibre 2.8 g; Cholesterol 246 mg; 1975 kJ (470 cal)

COOK'S FILE

SUGGESTED FISH: Orange roughy, snapper, red mullet, monkfish.

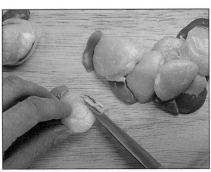

Cut off any vein, membrane or hard white muscle from each scallop.

When the mussels open, they are cooked. Discard any that don't open.

SMOKED HADDOCK CHOWDER

Preparation time: 20 minutes
Total cooking time: 35 minutes
Serves 4–6

500 g (1 lb 2 oz) smoked haddock
   or smoked cod
1 potato, diced
1 stick celery, diced
1 onion, finely chopped
50 g (1¾ oz) butter
1 rasher bacon, finely chopped
2 tablespoons plain (all-purpose) flour
½ teaspoon mustard powder
½ teaspoon Worcestershire
   sauce
250 ml (1 cup) milk
3 tablespoons chopped parsley
cream, for serving, optional

1 Put the fish in a deep frying pan, add 1.25 litres (5 cups) water and bring to the boil. Reduce the heat and simmer for 8 minutes, or until the fish flakes easily. Drain, reserving the liquid. Discard the skin and bones and flake the fish. Set aside.

2 Put the potato, celery and onion in a large saucepan with 750 ml (3 cups) of the reserved liquid. Bring to the boil, then reduce the heat and simmer for 8 minutes, or until the vegetables are tender. Set aside.

3 Melt the butter in a large saucepan over low heat, add the bacon and cook for 3 minutes. Stir in the flour, mustard powder and Worcestershire sauce and cook for 1 minute, or until the mixture is pale and foaming. Remove the saucepan from the heat and gradually stir in the milk. Return the pan to the heat and stir until the mixture boils and thickens. Reduce the heat and simmer for 2 minutes. Stir in the reserved vegetables and liquid, add the parsley and fish and simmer over low heat for 5 minutes, or until heated through. Season, to taste. If you wish, you can serve with a swirl of cream.

NUTRITION PER SERVE (6)
Protein 21.5 g; Fat 14.5 g; Carbohydrate 9 g; Dietary Fibre 1 g; Cholesterol 93 mg; 1058 kJ (254 cal)

Simmer the haddock in water until the fish flakes easily when tested with a fork.

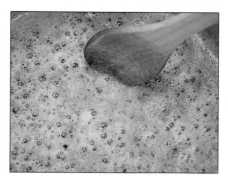
Stir with a wooden spoon until the flour mixture is pale and foaming.

When the milk is stirred through, return the pan to the heat and stir until thick.

CREAMY PRAWN BISQUE

Preparation time: 25 minutes
Total cooking time: 25 minutes
Serves 4–6

500 g (1 lb 2 oz) raw medium prawns (shrimp)
60 g (2¹/4 oz) butter
2 tablespoons plain (all-purpose) flour
2 litres (8 cups) fish stock
¹/2 teaspoon paprika
250 ml (1 cup) cream
80 ml (¹/3 cup) dry sherry
1–2 tablespoons cream, extra, for serving
paprika, extra, optional, to garnish

1 Peel the prawns and gently pull out the dark vein from each back, starting at the head end. Reserve the heads and shells. Melt the butter in a saucepan, add the prawn heads and shells and cook, stirring, over medium heat for 5 minutes, lightly crushing the heads with a wooden spoon.

2 Add the flour to the saucepan and stir until combined. Add the fish stock and paprika and stir until the mixture boils. Reduce the heat and simmer, covered, over low heat for 10 minutes. Strain the mixture through a fine sieve set over a bowl, then return the liquid to the saucepan. Discard the shells. Add the prawns to the saucepan and cook over low heat for 2–3 minutes. Cool slightly, then process in batches in a blender or food processor until smooth. Return the mixture to the saucepan.

3 Add the cream and sherry to the pan and stir to heat through. Season, to taste, with salt and freshly ground black pepper. Serve topped with a swirl of cream and sprinkled with paprika, if desired.

NUTRITION PER SERVE (6)
Protein 22.5 g; Fat 32 g; Carbohydrate 4 g; Dietary Fibre 0 g; Cholesterol 249.5 mg; 1679 kJ (400 cal)

COOK'S FILE

NOTE: The prawn heads and shells give the bisque its rich flavour. A few of the small cooked prawns can be reserved for garnishing.

Gently pull out the dark vein from each prawn back, starting at the head end.

Use a wooden spoon to lightly crush the prawn heads.

After cooking for 10 minutes, strain the mixture through a fine sieve into a bowl.

PRAWN LAKSA

Preparation time: 45 minutes
Total cooking time: 50 minutes
Serves 4

1 kg (2 lb 4 oz) raw medium prawns
    (shrimp)
80 ml (1/3 cup) oil
2–6 small fresh red chillies, seeded,
    finely chopped
1 onion, roughly chopped
3 cloves garlic, halved
2 cm x 2 cm (3/4 inch x 3/4 inch)
    piece fresh ginger or galangal,
    chopped
3 stems lemon grass, white
    part only, chopped
1 teaspoon ground turmeric
1 tablespoon ground coriander
2 teaspoons shrimp paste
625 g (2 1/2 cups) coconut cream
2 teaspoons grated palm sugar
    or soft brown sugar
4 fresh makrut (kaffir) lime leaves,
    crushed
1–2 tablespoons fish sauce
200 g (7 oz) packet fish balls
190 g (7 oz) packet fried tofu puffs
250 g (9 oz) dried rice vermicelli
125 g (4 1/2 oz) bean sprouts
20 g (1/3 cup) chopped mint,
    for serving
2 teaspoons coriander (cilantro)
    leaves, for serving

1 Peel the prawns and gently pull out the dark vein from each prawn back, starting at the head end. Reserve the shells and heads. Cover the prawn meat and refrigerate.
2 Heat 2 tablespoons of the oil in a wok or saucepan. Add the prawn heads and shells and stir over medium heat for 10 minutes, or until orange, then add 1 litre (4 cups) water. Bring to the boil, then reduce the heat and simmer for 15 minutes. Strain the stock, discarding the shells. Clean the pan.
3 Finely chop the chillies (use 2 for mild flavour, increase for hot), onion, garlic, ginger and lemon grass with the turmeric, coriander and 60 ml (1/4 cup) prawn stock in a processor.
4 Heat the remaining oil in the pan, add the chilli mixture and shrimp paste and stir over medium heat for 3 minutes, or until fragrant. Pour in the remaining stock and simmer for 10 minutes. Add the coconut cream, sugar, lime leaves and fish sauce and simmer for 5 minutes. Add the prawns and simmer for 2 minutes, or until firm and light pink. Add the fish balls and tofu puffs and simmer gently until just heated through.
5 Soak the rice vermicelli in boiling water for 2 minutes, drain and divide among 4 serving bowls. Top with the bean sprouts and soup. Sprinkle with the mint and coriander.

NUTRITION PER SERVE
Protein 58 g; Fat 58 g; Carbohydrate 71 g;
Dietary Fibre 9 g; Cholesterol 514 mg;
4331 kJ (1031 cal)

Stir and toss the prawn heads, shells and tails until the heads turn bright orange.

Process the chilli, onion, garlic, ginger, spices, lemon grass and stock.

Add the prawns to the pan and simmer until they turn light pink.

TOM YAM GOONG

Preparation time: 25 minutes
Total cooking time: 45 minutes
Serves 4–6

500 g (1 lb 2 oz) raw medium prawns (shrimp)
1 tablespoon oil
2 tablespoons tom yam paste
2 tablespoons tamarind purée
2 teaspoons ground turmeric
1 teaspoon chopped small red chillies
4 makrut (kaffir) lime leaves, shredded
2 tablespoons fish sauce
2 tablespoons lime juice
2 teaspoons grated palm sugar or soft brown sugar
makrut (kaffir) lime leaves, shredded, extra, to garnish

1 Peel the prawns, leaving the tails intact. Pull out the dark vein from each prawn back, starting at the head end. Reserve the shells and heads. Cover and refrigerate the prawn meat. Heat the oil in a wok or large saucepan and cook the shells and heads over medium heat, stirring frequently, for 10 minutes, or until the shells turn orange.

2 Add 250 ml (1 cup) water and the tom yam paste to the pan. Bring to the boil and cook for 5 minutes, or until reduced slightly. Add another 2 litres (8 cups) water, bring to the boil, reduce the heat and simmer for 20 minutes. Strain, discarding the shells and heads, and return the stock to the pan.

3 Add the tamarind, turmeric, chilli and lime leaves to the pan, bring to the boil and cook for 2 minutes. Add the prawns and cook for 5 minutes, or until pink. Stir in the fish sauce, lime juice and sugar. Garnish with shredded makrut lime leaves.

NUTRITION PER SERVE (6)
Protein 15 g; Fat 5 g; Carbohydrate 11 g; Dietary Fibre 1.3 g; Cholesterol 158 mg; 608 kJ (145 cal)

Finely shred the makrut lime leaves with a sharp knife.

Cook the water and tom yam paste until reduced slightly.

Stir in the tamarind, turmeric, chilli and lime leaves and cook for 2 minutes.

CORN AND CRAB SOUP

Preparation time: 15 minutes
Total cooking time: 10 minutes
Serves 4

1¹/2 tablespoons oil
6 cloves garlic, chopped
6 red Asian shallots, chopped
2 stems lemon grass, white
    part only, finely chopped
1 tablespoon grated fresh
    ginger
1 litre (4 cups) chicken stock
250 ml (1 cup) coconut milk
375 g (2¹/2 cups) frozen corn
    kernels
2 x 170 g (6 oz) cans crab meat,
    drained
2 tablespoons fish sauce
2 tablespoons lime juice
1 teaspoon shaved palm sugar
    or soft brown sugar

1 Heat the oil in a large saucepan, then add the chopped garlic, shallots and lemon grass and the grated ginger and cook, stirring, over medium heat for 2 minutes.

2 Pour the chicken stock and coconut milk into the saucepan and bring to the boil, stirring occasionally. Add the corn kernels and continue to cook for 5 minutes.

3 Add the drained crab meat, fish sauce, lime juice and sugar to the saucepan and stir until the crab is heated through. Season with salt and black pepper, to taste. Ladle into bowls and serve immediately.

NUTRITION PER SERVE
Protein 15 g; Fat 11 g; Carbohydrate 21.5 g;
Dietary Fibre 3.5 g; Cholesterol 71.5 mg;
1016 kJ (240 cal)

Peel off the outer layers of the Asian shallots before chopping.

Shave off thin slices of the palm sugar with a sharp knife.

When the soup comes to the boil, add the corn kernels and cook for 5 minutes.

FISH SOUP WITH SALSA

Preparation time: 30 minutes
    + 10 minutes cooling
Total cooking time: 30 minutes
Serves 4

40 g (1¹/2 oz) butter
2 leeks, finely sliced
50 g (¹/3 cup) finely chopped
    carrot
70 g (¹/2 cup) finely chopped
    celery
500 g (1 lb 2 oz) potatoes, peeled
    and diced
1.5 litres (6 cups) fish stock
1 bay leaf
300 g (10¹/2 oz) boneless, skinless
    firm white fish fillets, cut into
    bite-sized cubes
185 ml (³/4 cup) cream

Salsa
2 Roma (plum) tomatoes, peeled,
    seeded and finely diced
1 tablespoon finely chopped chives
1 clove garlic, crushed
2 teaspoons lime juice

1 Melt the butter in a large saucepan, add the leek, carrot and celery and stir over low heat for 5 minutes, or until the vegetables are soft but not brown. Add the potato, stock and bay leaf and bring to the boil. Reduce the heat and simmer, covered, for 20 minutes. Leave to cool for 10 minutes and remove the bay leaf.

2 For the salsa, stir the ingredients together in a small bowl, then season with salt and black pepper.

3 Blend the soup in batches in a blender or food processor until smooth. Return to the pan, bring to the boil and add the fish. Reduce the heat and simmer for 1 minute, or until the fish flakes easily. Stir in the cream and gently heat the soup without boiling. Season, to taste.

4 Divide the soup among heated bowls, top with a spoonful of the salsa and serve immediately.

NUTRITION PER SERVE
Protein 29 g; Fat 33.5 g; Carbohydrate
22.5 g; Dietary Fibre 5 g; Cholesterol
142.5 mg; 2120 kJ (505 cal)

COOK'S FILE

SUGGESTED FISH: Ling, bream.

Remove the bay leaf, then blend the cooled soup in batches until smooth.

To make the salsa, toss all the ingredients together in a small bowl.

SEAFOOD RAVIOLI IN GINGERY SOUP

Preparation time: 30 minutes
Total cooking time: 25 minutes
Serves 4

8 raw medium prawns (shrimp)
1 carrot, chopped
1 onion, chopped
1 celery stick, chopped
3 spring onions (scallions), thinly sliced
6 cm (2¹/2 inch) fresh ginger, shredded
1 tablespoon mirin
1 teaspoon kecap manis
1 tablespoon soy sauce
4 large scallops
100 g (3¹/2 oz) boneless white fish
    fillets

1 egg white, lightly beaten
32 gow gee wrappers

1 Peel the prawns, reserving the heads and shells. Pull out the vein from each back, starting at the head. Reserve 4 prawns and chop the rest into small pieces. Cover and refrigerate. Cook the heads and shells in a saucepan over high heat until orange, then cover with 1 litre (4 cups) water. Add the carrot, onion and celery, bring to the boil, then reduce the heat and simmer for 10 minutes. Strain and return the liquid to a clean pan. Add the spring onion, ginger, mirin, kecap manis and soy sauce.
2 Slice or pull off any vein, membrane or hard white muscle from each scallop and process with the whole

prawns and fish until smooth. Add enough egg white to bind. Lay half the wrappers on a work surface and place a rounded teaspoon of filling in the centre of each. Brush the edges with water. Top each with a wrapper and press the edges to seal. Trim with a fluted cutter. Cover to keep moist.
3 Heat the stock mixture and leave simmering. Bring a pan of water to the boil and cook a few ravioli at a time for 2 minutes. Divide among 4 bowls. Cook the chopped prawns in the same water for 2 minutes, then drain. Ladle the stock over the ravioli. Sprinkle with the prawns.

NUTRITION PER SERVE
Protein 21.5 g; Fat 2 g; Carbohydrate 32.5 g;
Dietary Fibre 2.5 g; Cholesterol 83 mg;
995 kJ (235 cal)

Peel the ginger and cut into fine shreds using a sharp knife.

Put filling in the centre of each wrapper and brush the edges with water.

When the ravioli are tender, remove from the water with a slotted spoon.

COCONUT PRAWN SOUP

Preparation time: 20 minutes
  + 15 minutes soaking
Total cooking time: 45 minutes
Serves 4

Curry Paste
6 long dried red chillies
1 teaspoon cumin seeds
2 teaspoons coriander seeds
1/2 teaspoon paprika
1 teaspoon ground turmeric
1/2 teaspoon black peppercorns
4 red Asian shallots, chopped
4 cloves garlic, roughly chopped
2 cm x 2 cm (3/4 inch x 3/4 inch)
    piece fresh ginger, sliced
4 fresh coriander (cilantro) roots
2 tablespoons chopped coriander
    (cilantro) stems
1 teaspoon grated lime zest
2 stems lemon grass, white part
    only, sliced
2 makrut (kaffir) lime leaves, shredded
1 teaspoon shrimp paste
2 tablespoons oil

Stock
700 g (1 lb 9 oz) raw medium prawns
    (shrimp)
4 red Asian shallots, chopped
1 clove garlic
grassy ends of lemon grass
6 black peppercorns

2 tablespoons oil
2 x 400 ml (14 fl oz) cans coconut milk
60 ml (1/4 cup) fish sauce
coriander (cilantro) leaves, to garnish
lime zest, cut in strips, to garnish

1 For the curry paste, soak the chillies in boiling water for 10–15 minutes, then drain. Toss the spices and

peppercorns in a dry frying pan over medium heat for 1 minute, or until fragrant. Grind to a powder in a spice grinder or mortar and pestle, then transfer to a food processor and add the remaining paste ingredients and 1 teaspoon salt. Process until smooth. Add a little water, if necessary.

2 Peel the prawns, leaving the tails intact. Gently pull out the vein from each prawn back, starting at the head end. Cover and refrigerate. Reserve the heads and shells.

3 For the stock, dry-fry the prawn heads and shells in a wok or large saucepan over high heat for 5 minutes until orange. Add the remaining stock ingredients and 1.5 litres (6 cups)

water and bring to the boil. Reduce the heat, simmer for 15–20 minutes, then strain, reserving the liquid.

4 Heat the oil in a wok and add 3 tablespoons curry paste (freeze the leftover in an airtight container) and stir constantly over medium heat for 1–2 minutes, until fragrant. Stir in the stock and coconut milk. Bring to the boil, then reduce the heat and simmer for 10 minutes. Add the prawns and cook, stirring, for 2 minutes, or until the prawns are cooked. Stir in the fish sauce and garnish to your liking.

NUTRITION PER SERVE
Protein 38.5 g; Fat 60 g; Carbohydrate 11.5 g; Dietary Fibre 3 g; Cholesterol 355 mg; 2972 kJ (705 cal)

Grind the cumin and coriander seeds, paprika, turmeric and peppercorns.

Process the ground spices with the remaining paste ingredients until smooth.

Simmer the stock for 15–20 minutes to reduce the liquid.

MUSSEL AND LEEK SOUP

Preparation time: 20 minutes
  + 15 minutes cooling
Total cooking time: 35 minutes
Serves 4

2 tablespoons light olive oil
2 cloves garlic, finely chopped
2 leeks, sliced
250 g (9 oz) desirée potatoes, diced
1 litre (4 cups) fish or vegetable stock
1.5 kg (3 lb 5 oz) black mussels
250 ml (1 cup) white wine
3 tablespoons chopped flat-leaf
    (Italian) parsley
1 tablespoon lemon juice

1 Heat the oil in a large saucepan, add the garlic and leek and stir over medium heat for 2–3 minutes, or until the leek is soft but not brown. Add the potato and stir for 1 minute. Add the stock and bring to the boil. Reduce the heat, cover and simmer for 20 minutes.
2 Scrub the mussels with a stiff brush and pull out the hairy beards. Discard any broken mussels, or open ones that don't close when tapped on the bench. Rinse well. Place the mussels in a large saucepan with the wine and 250 ml (1 cup) water. Cover and slowly bring to the boil. Reduce the heat and simmer for 5 minutes, or until the mussels open. Remove the mussels with tongs, draining any liquid back into the saucepan, and place in a large bowl. Discard any unopened mussels.
3 Strain the mussel liquid through a fine sieve lined with muslin and return the liquid to the pan. Process the potato and leek mixture in batches in a blender or food processor until smooth. Pour into the saucepan with

the mussel liquid and gently reheat without boiling. Stir in the mussels, parsley and lemon juice. Season, to taste. Serve immediately.

NUTRITION PER SERVE
Protein 48.5 g; Fat 18.5 g; Carbohydrate 31 g; Dietary Fibre 4.5 g; Cholesterol 105 mg; 2240 kJ (535 cal)

After scrubbing the mussel shells thoroughly, pull out the hairy beards.

Simmer the liquid until the mussels open, discarding any that don't open.

Strain the mussel liquid through a sieve lined with muslin or other clean cloth.

TOMATO SEAFOOD SOUP

Preparation time: 15 minutes
Total cooking time: 35 minutes
Serves 4–6

2 tablespoons olive oil
2 leeks, finely sliced
1 stick celery, finely sliced
2 cloves garlic, crushed
250 g (9 oz) desirée potatoes, cut
   into bite-sized cubes
100 g (3^1/2 oz) sun-dried tomatoes,
   drained, chopped
400 g (14 oz) can diced tomatoes
1.25 litres (5 cups) fish stock
2 teaspoons sugar
350 g (12 oz) firm white fish fillets
250 g (9 oz) raw medium prawns
   (shrimp)
2 tablespoons parsley, finely chopped

1 Heat the oil in a large saucepan, add the leek, celery and garlic and cook over medium heat for 2–3 minutes, or until softened. Add the potato and sun-dried tomato and stir for 1–2 minutes. Add the diced tomato, stock and sugar. Bring slowly to the boil, then reduce the heat and simmer, covered, for 15 minutes.

2 Meanwhile, remove any skin and bones from the fish fillets and cut the fillets into bite-sized cubes. Peel the prawns and gently pull out the dark vein from each prawn back, starting at the head end.

3 Add the fish to the saucepan and simmer gently for 5 minutes, or until nearly cooked. Add the prawns and cook for 3 minutes, or until cooked. Season with salt and freshly ground black pepper and stir in the chopped parsley. Serve with crusty bread.

NUTRITION PER SERVE (6)
Protein 43.5 g; Fat 17.5 g; Carbohydrate 10.5 g; Dietary Fibre 3 g; Cholesterol 129.5 mg; 1591 kJ (379 cal)

COOK'S FILE

SUGGESTED FISH: Ling, gemfish, snapper, hake.

Stir in the potato and sun-dried tomato for 1–2 minutes.

Remove any remaining skin and bones from the fish and cut into cubes.

STARTERS & FINGER FOOD

SMOKED FISH PATE WITH BRUSCHETTA

Preparation time: 20 minutes
  + several hours refrigeration
Total cooking time: 15 minutes
Serves 8

2 x 400 g (14 oz) smoked rainbow
  trout fillets
2–3 tablespoons lemon or
  lime juice
125 g (4½ oz) cream cheese,
  softened
200 g (7 oz) butter, melted
sprigs of herbs such as dill,
  fennel or flat-leaf (Italian)
  parsley, to garnish
lemon slices, to garnish

Bruschetta
1 bread stick, sliced
  diagonally into
  24 thin slices
80 ml (⅓ cup) olive oil
3 cloves garlic

1 Remove the skin and bones from the fish and roughly flake the flesh. Process the flesh in a blender or food processor with the juice, cream cheese and melted butter until the mixture is quite smooth. Season, to taste, with freshly ground black pepper.

2 Spoon into eight 60 ml (¼ cup) ramekins and refrigerate for 2 hours, or overnight, until the mixture has firmed. Keep refrigerated until ready to serve. Garnish with sprigs of fresh herbs and lemon slices.

3 For the bruschetta, preheat the oven to 200°C (400°F/Gas 6). Brush both sides of the bread slices lightly with oil, then spread out on a baking tray and bake for about 10–15 minutes, until crisp and golden, turning over once. Remove and rub all over one side of each slice with a garlic clove, using a clove for every 8 slices.

NUTRITION PER SERVE
Protein 29.5 g; Fat 42 g; Carbohydrate 18.5 g; Dietary Fibre 1 g; Cholesterol 157 mg; 2385 kJ (570 cal)

Process the flaked fish, juice, cream cheese and butter until smooth.

After baking the bread, rub one side of each slice with garlic.

DEEP-FRIED PRAWN TOASTS WITH WASABI MAYONNAISE

Preparation time: 45 minutes
Total cooking time: 25 minutes
Makes 25

Wasabi Mayonnaise
125 g (½ cup) whole-egg
   mayonnaise
1 teaspoon wasabi paste
2 teaspoons Japanese soy sauce

1 loaf day-old unsliced white bread
25 small raw prawns (shrimp)
3 sheets nori (dried seaweed)
3 eggs
80 g (½ cup) sesame seeds
oil, for deep-frying

1 Mix all the wasabi mayonnaise ingredients in a small bowl, then cover and refrigerate.
2 Remove the crusts from the bread and cut the bread into 3 cm (1¼ inch) cubes (to give 25). Peel the prawns, leaving the tails intact. Gently pull out the dark vein from each prawn back, starting at the head end.
3 Using a sharp knife, make an incision in the top of each bread cube to about three-quarters of the way through. Gently ease a prawn, tail-end out, into each slit in the bread cubes. Cut 25 strips from the nori sheets, measuring 2 x 15 cm (¾ x 6 inches). Wrap a strip around the outside of each bread cube and secure each with a toothpick. Lightly beat the eggs in a small bowl and put the sesame seeds in a separate bowl. Dip the bread cubes in egg, draining off any excess, then coat in the sesame seeds (leave the prawn tails uncoated if you wish).
4 Fill a wok or a deep saucepan one third full of oil and heat to 180°C (350°F), or until a small cube of bread browns in 15 seconds. Deep-fry batches of the prawn toasts for 1–2 minutes, or until the bread is golden and the prawns are pink and cooked. Drain on paper towels and season with salt. Remove the toothpicks and serve with the wasabi mayonnaise.

NUTRITION PER PIECE
Protein 28 g; Fat 4 g; Carbohydrate 13 g;
Dietary Fibre 1 g; Cholesterol 48 mg;
510 kJ (120 cal)

Hold the bread firmly and ease a prawn into the slit in each cube of bread.

Wrap nori around each bread cube and thread a toothpick through to secure.

Dip the cubes in egg, drain off any excess, then coat in sesame seeds.

Deep-fry the cubes until the prawns are pink and cooked through.

WHITEBAIT FRITTERS

Preparation time: 25 minutes
Total cooking time: 10 minutes
Makes 25

Garlic Mayonnaise
125 g (½ cup) whole-egg
    mayonnaise
2 cloves garlic, crushed
1 tablespoon extra virgin olive oil
1 tablespoon lime juice

500 g (1 lb 2 oz) whitebait
125 g (1 cup) plain (all-purpose)
    flour

¾ teaspoon cayenne pepper
2 tablespoons finely chopped
    basil
250 ml (1 cup) chilled soda water
oil, for deep-frying

1 Stir all the garlic mayonnaise ingredients together in a small bowl. Refrigerate until ready to use.
2 Rinse the whitebait under cold water, then drain. Remove the heads and tails and cut each body into three.
3 Sift the flour, cayenne, ¼ teaspoon salt and a pinch of cracked black pepper into a large bowl. Stir in the fresh basil and make a well in the centre. Gradually add the soda water,

mixing to make a smooth, lump-free batter. Fold the whitebait pieces through the batter.
4 Fill a wok or a deep saucepan one third full of oil and heat to 180°C (350°F), or until a cube of bread dropped in the oil browns in 15 seconds. Cook heaped tablespoons of the prepared batter in batches for 1–2 minutes, or until golden and cooked through. Drain on crumpled paper towels and season with salt. Serve with the garlic mayonnaise.

NUTRITION PER PIECE
Protein 5 g; Fat 3 g; Carbohydrate 4.5 g;
Dietary Fibre 0.5 g; Cholesterol 15.5 mg;
270 kJ (65 cal)

Cut the head and tail off each whitebait, then cut each body into three pieces.

When the batter is smooth, add the pieces of whitebait and fold through.

Remove the cooked fritters from the hot oil with a slotted spoon.

MINI SALMON AND CAMEMBERT QUICHES

Preparation time: 30 minutes
 + 1 hour refrigeration + cooling
Total cooking time: 30 minutes
Makes 24

Pastry
250 g (2 cups) plain (all-purpose) flour
150 g (5½ oz) butter, chopped
2 egg yolks, lightly beaten
½ teaspoon paprika

Filling
1 tablespoon olive oil
2 small leeks, finely sliced
75 g (2½ oz) smoked salmon, sliced
80 g (2½ oz) camembert, chopped
2 eggs, lightly beaten
125 ml (½ cup) cream
2 teaspoons grated lemon zest
1 teaspoon chopped dill
1 tablespoon finely chopped chives,
    for serving

1 Sift the flour into a large bowl and rub in the butter with your fingertips until the mixture resembles fine breadcrumbs. Make a well, add the egg, paprika and 1 teaspoon water and mix with a flat-bladed knife, using a cutting action, until the mixture comes together in beads. Gently gather together and lift onto a lightly floured work surface. Press together into a ball, wrap in plastic wrap and refrigerate for 30 minutes.
2 Grease two 12-hole patty tins. Divide the pastry into 4 pieces. Roll each between 2 sheets of baking paper to 2 mm (⅛ inch) thick. Cut 24 rounds using a 7 cm (2¾ inch) fluted cutter. Lift the rounds into the patty tins, pressing into shape but being careful

not to stretch the pastry. Refrigerate for 30 minutes.
3 Preheat the oven to 180°C (350°F/ Gas 4). Bake the pastry for 5 minutes, or until lightly golden. If the pastry has puffed up, press down lightly with a tea towel.
4 For the filling, heat the oil in a frying pan and cook the leek for 2–3 minutes, or until soft. Remove from the pan and cool. Divide the leek, smoked salmon and camembert pieces evenly among the pastry cases.

5 Whisk the eggs, cream, lemon zest and dill together in a jug, then pour some into each pastry. Bake for 15–20 minutes, or until lightly golden and set. Serve sprinkled with chives.

NUTRITION PER QUICHE
Protein 3.5 g; Fat 10 g; Carbohydrate 8 g; Dietary Fibre 0.5 g; Cholesterol 57.5 mg; 570 kJ (135 cal)

COOK'S FILE

NOTE: You can substitute crab meat or small prawns (shrimp) for the salmon.

Cut the rounds and lift into the patty tins, gently pressing into shape.

Bake the pastry rounds for 5 minutes, or until lightly golden.

Pour some of the egg, cream, lemon rind and dill mixture into each pastry case.

WON TON WRAPPED PRAWNS

Preparation time: 20 minutes
  + 20 minutes refrigeration
Total cooking time: 10 minutes
Makes 24

24 raw medium prawns (shrimp)
1 teaspoon cornflour (cornstarch)
24 won ton wrappers
oil, for deep-frying
125 ml (1/2 cup) sweet chilli
    sauce
1 tablespoon lime juice

1 Peel the prawns, leaving the tails intact. Pull out the dark vein from each back, starting at the head end.
2 Mix the cornflour with 1 teaspoon water in a small bowl. Fold each won ton wrapper in half to form a triangle. Cover them with a tea towel while you are working, to prevent them drying out. Wrap each prawn in a wrapper, leaving the tail exposed. Seal at the end by brushing on a little of the cornflour mixture, then pressing gently. Spread the wrapped prawns on a baking tray, cover with plastic wrap and refrigerate for 20 minutes.
3 Fill a deep heavy-based saucepan one third full of oil and heat to 180°C (350°F), or until a cube of bread dropped into the oil browns in 15 seconds. Cook the prawns in batches for 1½ minutes each batch, or until crisp, golden and cooked through. The cooking time may vary depending on the size of the prawns. Determine the time by cooking one prawn and testing it before continuing. Remove the prawns from the oil with a slotted spoon and drain on crumpled paper towels.
4 Stir the sweet chilli sauce and lime juice together in a small bowl. Serve with the prawns.

NUTRITION PER PRAWN
Protein 4.5 g; Fat 2 g; Carbohydrate 5.5 g;
Dietary Fibre 0.5 g; Cholesterol 27 mg;
245 kJ (60 cal)

Seal the wrapped prawns at the end with a dab of cornflour mixture.

Remove the cooked prawns using a slotted spoon.

SMOKED SALMON AND GOATS CHEESE PIKELETS

Preparation time: 25 minutes
+ 30 minutes standing
Total cooking time: 10 minutes
Makes 30

60 g (2¼ oz) goats cheese
50 g (1¾ cup) smoked salmon
90 g (¾ cup) self-raising flour
1 egg
250 ml (1 cup) milk
20 g (¾ oz) butter, melted
60 g (¼ cup) crème fraîche
3 tablespoons salmon roe
dill sprigs, to garnish

Crumble the goats cheese into smallish pieces with your fingers.

1 Crumble the goats cheese into small pieces with your fingers. Chop the smoked salmon into small pieces. Sift the flour into a bowl and make a well in the centre. Whisk the egg, milk and butter in a jug and pour into the well, whisking until smooth. Cover and set aside for 30 minutes. Stir in the goats cheese and smoked salmon.
2 Heat a frying pan and brush the base lightly with melted butter. Drop teaspoons of batter into the pan and cook over medium heat for 1 minute, or until small bubbles begin to appear on the surface and the underside is golden. Turn the pikelets over and cook for 1 minute. Transfer to a plate and cover while cooking the rest.

Stir the goats cheese and salmon into the pikelet mixture.

3 When ready to serve, spoon a little of the crème fraîche onto each pikelet, then top each with some salmon roe. Garnish each with a sprig of dill and season with salt and pepper, to taste. Arrange on a platter.

NUTRITION PER PIECE
Protein 2 g; Fat 2.5 g; Carbohydrate 2.5 g; Dietary Fibre 0.5 g; Cholesterol 20 mg; 175 kJ (40 cal)

COOK'S FILE

NOTE: If you wish, you can cook the pikelets a day in advance and store them in an airtight container in the refrigerator. For full flavour, allow the pikelets to return to room temperature before serving.

When small bubbles appear on the surface, turn the pikelets over.

CRAB AND VERMICELLI CUCUMBER BOATS

Preparation time: 30 minutes
+ 5 minutes standing + refrigeration
Total cooking time: Nil
Makes 30

6 even-sized 4 cm (1½ inch) diameter Lebanese (short) cucumbers
50 g (1¾ oz) dried rice vermicelli
2 x 170 g (6 oz) cans crab meat
60 ml (¼ cup) lime juice
2 tablespoons sweet chilli sauce
3 tablespoons finely chopped coriander (cilantro)
1 small makrut (kaffir) lime leaf, finely shredded
2 teaspoons fish sauce

1 Trim the ends from the cucumbers and cut into 2.5 cm (1 inch) chunks. Using a small melon baller, scoop out the centre of the cucumber chunks three-quarters of the way through.

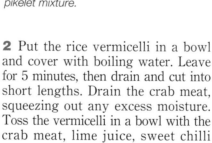

Use a small melon baller to scoop out the centre of the cucumber chunks.

2 Put the rice vermicelli in a bowl and cover with boiling water. Leave for 5 minutes, then drain and cut into short lengths. Drain the crab meat, squeezing out any excess moisture. Toss the vermicelli in a bowl with the crab meat, lime juice, sweet chilli sauce, coriander, shredded makrut lime leaf and fish sauce.
3 Spoon teaspoons of the vermicelli mixture into the hollows in the chunks of cucumber. Spoon any remaining

sauce over the cucumber, then cover and refrigerate until ready to serve.

NUTRITION PER PIECE
Protein 1.5 g; Fat 0.5 g; Carbohydrate 2 g; Dietary Fibre 0.5 g; Cholesterol 8.5 mg; 68 kJ (16 cal)

COOK'S FILE

NOTE: It is better not to make these more than 3 hours before you need them as the cucumber may tend to dry out.

Toss the vermicelli with the other ingredients using two spoons.

STEAMED PRAWN NORI ROLLS

Preparation time: 15 minutes
 + 1 hour refrigeration
Total cooking time: 5 minutes
Makes 25

500 g (1 lb 2 oz) peeled raw prawns
  (shrimp), deveined
1½ tablespoons fish sauce
1 tablespoon sake
2 tablespoons chopped coriander
  (cilantro)
1 large fresh makrut (kaffir) lime leaf,
  finely shredded
1 tablespoon lime juice

2 teaspoons sweet chilli sauce
1 egg white, lightly beaten
5 sheets nori

Dipping Sauce
60 ml (¼ cup) sake
60 ml (¼ cup) soy sauce
1 tablespoon mirin
1 tablespoon lime juice

1 Process the prawns in a food processor or blender with the fish sauce, sake, coriander, lime leaf, lime juice and sweet chilli sauce, until smooth. Add the egg white and pulse for a few seconds to just combine.
2 Lay the nori sheets on a flat surface and spread some prawn mixture over

each sheet, leaving a 2 cm (¾ inch) border at one end. Roll up tightly, cover and refrigerate for 1 hour to firm. Using a sharp knife, trim the ends, then cut into 2 cm (¾ inch) lengths.
3 Place the rolls in a lined bamboo steamer. Cover the steamer and place it over a wok of simmering water, making sure it doesn't touch the water. Steam the rolls for 5 minutes, or until heated thoroughly.
4 For the dipping sauce, thoroughly mix all the ingredients together in a small bowl. Serve with the nori rolls.

NUTRITION PER PIECE
Protein 4 g; Fat 0.5 g; Carbohydrate 0.5 g;
Dietary Fibre 0.5 g; Cholesterol 39.5 mg;
95 kJ (23 cal)

Spread prawn mixture over each nori sheet, leaving a border at one end.

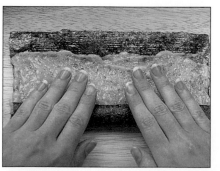

Roll each sheet up tightly, then cover and refrigerate to firm.

Cut the nori rolls into short lengths with a very sharp knife.

SMOKED SALMON BREAD BASKETS

Preparation time: 20 minutes + cooling
Total cooking time: 10 minutes
Makes 24

1 loaf white sliced bread
60 ml (¼ cup) olive oil
90 g (⅓ cup) whole-egg
    mayonnaise
2 teaspoons extra virgin olive oil
1 teaspoon white wine vinegar
1 teaspoon finely chopped dill
3 teaspoons horseradish cream
250 g (9 oz) smoked salmon, cut
    into 2 cm (¾ inch) wide strips
3 tablespoons salmon roe
dill sprigs, to garnish

1 Preheat the oven to 180°C (350°F/ Gas 4). Flatten the bread to 1 mm (¹⁄₁₆ inch) with a rolling pin, then cut 24 rounds with a 7 cm (2¾ inch) cutter. Brush both sides of the rounds with olive oil and push into the holes of two 12-hole flat-based patty tins. Bake for 10 minutes, or until crisp. Allow the bread baskets to cool.
2 Stir the mayonnaise in a bowl with the extra virgin olive oil, vinegar, dill and horseradish until combined.
3 Arrange folds of salmon in each cooled bread case and top each with 1 teaspoon of mayonnaise mixture. Spoon ½ teaspoon of salmon roe on top of each, garnish with dill and serve.

NUTRITION PER PIECE
Protein 5.5 g; Fat 5.5 g; Carbohydrate 14 g; Dietary Fibre 1 g; Cholesterol 15 mg; 530 kJ (125 cal)

COOK'S FILE

NOTE: The bread cases can be made a day in advance and when completely cold, stored in an airtight container. If they soften, you can crisp them on a baking tray in a 180°C (350°F/Gas 4) oven for 5 minutes. Cool before filling.

Gently push the oiled rounds into the patty tin holes.

Fold the strips of salmon to fit into the cooled bread cases.

PRAWN COCKTAILS

Preparation time: 20 minutes
Total cooking time: Nil
Serves 6

Cocktail Sauce
250 g (1 cup) whole-egg
      mayonnaise
60 ml (¼ cup) tomato sauce
2 teaspoons Worcestershire sauce
½ teaspoon lemon juice
1 drop Tabasco sauce

1 kg (2 lb 4 oz) cooked medium
      prawns (shrimp)
lettuce, for serving
lemon wedges, for serving
sliced bread, for serving

1 For the cocktail sauce, mix all the ingredients together in a bowl, then season with salt and pepper.
2 Peel the prawns, leaving some with tails intact to use as a garnish. Remove the tails from the rest. Gently pull out the dark vein from each prawn back, starting at the head end. Add the prawns without tails to the sauce and mix to coat.
3 Arrange lettuce in serving dishes or bowls. Spoon some prawns into each dish. Garnish with the reserved prawns, drizzling with some dressing. Serve with lemon wedges and bread.

NUTRITION PER SERVE
Protein 42.5 g; Fat 16 g; Carbohydrate 34 g; Dietary Fibre 4 g; Cholesterol 311 mg; 1900 kJ (454 cal)

COOK'S FILE

NOTE: You can make the cocktail sauce several hours ahead and refrigerate. Stir in 2 tablespoons of thick cream for a creamier sauce.

Mix all the cocktail sauce ingredients together in a bowl.

Carefully pull the shells off the prawns, leaving the tails intact.

Put the prawns in with the cocktail sauce and mix gently until well coated.

CHARGRILLED BABY OCTOPUS

Preparation time: 15 minutes
+ overnight marinating
Total cooking time: 10 minutes
Serves 4

1 kg (2 lb 4 oz) baby octopus
185 ml (¾ cup) red wine
2 tablespoons balsamic vinegar
2 tablespoons soy sauce
2 tablespoons hoisin sauce
1 clove garlic, crushed

1 Cut off the octopus heads, below the eyes, with a sharp knife. Discard the heads and guts. Push the beaks out with your index finger, remove and discard. Wash the octopus thoroughly under running water and drain on crumpled paper towels. If the octopus are large, cut the tentacles into quarters.

2 Put the octopus in a large bowl. Stir together the wine, vinegar, soy sauce, hoisin sauce and garlic in a jug and pour over the octopus. Toss to coat, then cover and refrigerate for several hours, or overnight.

3 Heat a chargrill plate or barbecue hotplate until very hot and then lightly grease. Drain the octopus, reserving the marinade. Cook in batches for 3–5 minutes, or until the octopus flesh turns white. Brush the marinade over the octopus during cooking. Be careful not to overcook or the octopus will be tough. Serve warm or cold. Delicious with a green salad and lime wedges.

NUTRITION PER SERVE
Protein 42.5 g; Fat 3.5 g; Carbohydrate 4 g;
Dietary Fibre 1 g; Cholesterol 497.5 mg;
1060 kJ (255 cal)

Remove and discard the head from each octopus using a sharp knife.

Push the beaks through the centre with your index finger.

Brush the octopus all over with the reserved marinade while cooking.

OYSTERS

Fresh oysters in the shell as served to us by nature are a sheer delight. However, these recipes show how to enhance nature's treats for special occasions. We have used 12 oysters for each recipe.

OYSTERS WITH SMOKED SALMON

Remove 12 oysters from their shells, reserving the shells. Divide 100 g (3½ oz) finely sliced smoked salmon among the shells. Return the oysters to the shells and drizzle each with ½ teaspoon lime juice. Spoon ½ teaspoon crème fraîche over each, then top with ¼ teaspoon salmon roe. Season with salt and freshly ground black pepper.

CHAMPAGNE OYSTERS

Melt 30 g (1 oz) butter in a small saucepan over medium heat. Add 2 tablespoons snipped chives and 375 ml (1½ cups) Champagne, then bring to the boil and boil for 5 minutes, or until reduced by half. Strain and return to the saucepan. Gradually whisk in 50 g (1¾ oz) cubed butter and simmer for 1 minute. Remove from the heat and divide among 12 oysters in shells, spooning over the top. Season with salt and freshly ground black pepper and sprinkle with chopped chives.

This page, from top: Oysters with smoked salmon; Champagne oysters; Crumbed oysters.
Opposite page, from top: Asian-flavoured oysters; Grilled oysters; Oysters ceviche.

CRUMBED OYSTERS

Place 60 g (1 cup) Japanese breadcrumbs in a bowl, cut a sheet of nori (dried seaweed) into small pieces with scissors and stir into the crumbs. Season some plain (all-purpose) flour with a little salt and pepper in a shallow bowl. Lightly beat an egg in a separate bowl. Remove 12 oysters from their shells, pat dry with paper towels and dust lightly with the flour. Dip into the beaten egg, allowing any excess to drain off, then coat in the breadcrumb mixture. Fill a deep heavy-based saucepan one third full of oil and heat to 180°C (350°F), or until a cube of bread dropped into the oil browns in 15 seconds. Cook the oysters in batches for 1 minute each batch, or until golden brown. Drain on crumpled paper towels. Return to the shells and serve hot.

ASIAN-FLAVOURED OYSTERS

Arrange 12 oysters in shells in a lined bamboo steamer. Divide among the oysters 2 finely chopped garlic cloves, 1 tablespoon julienned fresh ginger, 1 1/2 tablespoons finely chopped coriander (cilantro) and 2 spring onions (scallions), finely sliced on the diagonal. Spoon 1 teaspoon Japanese soy sauce over each oyster, cover the steamer and place over a wok of simmering water. Make sure the water is not touching the steamer. Steam for 2 minutes. Heat 60 ml (1/4 cup) peanut oil in a small saucepan until smoking and carefully spoon 1 teaspoon over each oyster. Serve immediately.

GRILLED OYSTERS

Process 6 slices fresh white bread, crusts removed, in a food processor or blender, together with 2 crushed garlic cloves, 4 tablespoons chopped basil, 2 tablespoons toasted pine nuts and 60 ml (1/4 cup) extra virgin olive oil until combined. Place 12 oysters in shells on a lined griller (broiler) tray and spoon 1 tablespoon of the crumb mixture evenly over each oyster. Cook under a moderate griller (broiler) for 1–2 minutes, or until golden. Serve with lemon wedges.

OYSTERS CEVICHE

Place 60 ml (1/4 cup) lime juice, 1 teaspoon finely grated lime zest, 2 crushed garlic cloves, 2 seeded, finely chopped small red chillies and 1 tablespoon each of finely chopped coriander (cilantro) and olive oil in a small bowl and mix well. Remove 12 oysters from their shells, reserving the shells, and place the oysters in the lime mixture, tossing to coat well. Cover and refrigerate for 2 hours. Peel 1 ripe tomato, remove the seeds and finely dice the flesh. Mix gently in a small bowl with 1/2 diced ripe avocado. Season with salt and freshly ground black pepper. Place the oysters back in the shells and spoon some lime mixture over each. Top with a teaspoon of the tomato salsa and serve.

SARDINES WITH HERB AND PARMESAN CRUST

Preparation time: 40 minutes
+ 30 minutes refrigeration
Total cooking time: 40 minutes
Serves 4

120 g (1½ cups) fresh breadcrumbs
50 g (½ cup) grated Parmesan
cheese
3 tablespoons chopped flat-leaf
(Italian) parsley
2 eggs
12 butterflied fresh sardines
125 ml (½ cup) light olive oil,
for pan-frying

Tomato and Olive Sauce
1 tablespoon olive oil
1 small onion, finely chopped
2 cloves garlic, finely chopped
410 g (14 oz) bottle tomato pasta sauce
250 ml (1 cup) chicken stock
1 teaspoon sugar
75 g (½ cup) pitted black olives,
chopped
2 tablespoons chopped basil

1 Mix the breadcrumbs, Parmesan and parsley in a bowl. Lightly beat the eggs in a separate bowl. Dip the sardines in the egg, drain off any excess, then coat with breadcrumb mixture. Place in a single layer on a tray or plate and chill for 30 minutes.
2 For the tomato and olive sauce, heat the oil in a saucepan, add the onion and garlic and cook over medium heat for 2–3 minutes, or until the onion is soft. Add the tomato sauce, stock and sugar. Bring to the boil, then reduce the heat and simmer, stirring occasionally, for 20 minutes, or until the sauce has thickened. Stir in the olives and basil.
3 Heat the light olive oil in a large frying pan, add the sardines and cook in batches for 2–3 minutes each side, or until golden brown and cooked through. Serve with the sauce.

NUTRITION PER SERVE
Protein 52 g; Fat 48.5 g; Carbohydrate 35 g; Dietary Fibre 5 g; Cholesterol 227 mg; 3270 kJ (780 cal)

COOK'S FILE

ALTERNATIVE FISH: Garfish, red-spot whiting, redfish.

Coat the sardines with the breadcrumb mixture and refrigerate for 30 minutes.

Meanwhile, for the tomato and olive sauce, finely chop the small onion.

Simmer the sauce until thickened, stirring occasionally with a wooden spoon.

Cook the sardines in batches until golden brown and cooked through.

SCALLOP AND PRAWN TIMBALES WITH SAFFRON CREAM SAUCE

Preparation time: 30 minutes
Total cooking time: 35 minutes
Serves 4

375 g (13 oz) small raw prawns (shrimp)
250 g (9 oz) scallops
1 egg, plus 1 egg yolk
125 g (4½ oz) ricotta
2 tablespoons lemon juice
125 ml (½ cup) cream

Saffron Cream Sauce
30 g (1 oz) butter
2 teaspoons plain (all-purpose) flour

185 ml (¾ cup) chicken stock
125 ml (½ cup) cream
¼ teaspoon saffron threads
1 tablespoon snipped chives

1 Preheat the oven to 160°C (315°F/ Gas 2–3). Grease four 185 ml (¾ cup) ovenproof dishes.
2 Peel the prawns and pull out the dark vein from each prawn back, starting at the head. Slice or pull off any vein, membrane or hard muscle from the scallops, leaving roe attached.
3 Process the prawns, scallops, egg, egg yolk, ricotta, lemon juice, cream and ½ teaspoon salt in a processor and blend until smooth. Divide among the dishes, then cover with foil. Place in a baking dish and pour boiling water into the dish to come

halfway up the sides of the dishes. Bake for 30–35 minutes, or until the timbales shrink from the edges and are firm when tested with a skewer. Run a knife around the edges of the timbales, drain away any liquid, then turn out and serve with the sauce.
4 While the timbales are cooking, make the sauce. Melt the butter in a small saucepan, add the flour and stir for 1 minute, or until pale and foaming, then remove from the heat. Gradually stir in the stock, cream and saffron. Return to the heat, stirring constantly, until the sauce boils and thickens. Season and stir in the chives.

NUTRITION PER SERVE
Protein 30.5 g; Fat 40 g; Carbohydrate 4 g; Dietary Fibre 0 g; Cholesterol 406.5 mg; 2065 kJ (495 cal)

Divide the mixture evenly among the ovenproof dishes.

Bake until the timbales are firm when tested with a skewer.

Stir constantly with a wooden spoon until the sauce boils and thickens.

SALT-AND-PEPPER SQUID

Preparation time: 30 minutes
  + 15 minutes marinating
Total cooking time: 10 minutes
Serves 6

1 kg (2 lb 4 oz) squid hoods, halved
    lengthways
250 ml (1 cup) lemon juice
125 g (1 cup) cornflour (cornstarch)
1½ tablespoons salt
1 tablespoon ground white pepper
2 teaspoons caster (superfine)
    sugar

4 egg whites, lightly beaten
oil, for deep-frying
coriander (cilantro) sprigs, to garnish
lemon wedges, for serving

1 Open out the squid hoods, wash and pat dry. Score a shallow diamond pattern on the inside, then cut into 5 cm x 3 cm (2 inch x 1¼ inch) pieces. Place in a flat non-metallic dish and pour on the lemon juice. Cover and refrigerate for 15 minutes. Drain well and pat dry.
2 Combine the cornflour, salt, white pepper and sugar in a bowl. Dip the squid into the egg white and lightly coat with the cornflour mixture, shaking off any excess.
3 Fill a deep heavy-based pan one third full of oil and heat to 180°C (350°F), or until a cube of bread dropped into the oil turns golden brown in 15 seconds. Deep-fry the squid, in batches, for 1 minute each batch, or until the squid turns white and curls up. Drain on crumpled paper towels. Garnish with coriander sprigs and serve with lemon wedges.

NUTRITION PER SERVE
Protein 30.5 g; Fat 8.5 g; Carbohydrate 22 g; Dietary Fibre 0.5 g; Cholesterol 331.5 mg; 1225 kJ (290 cal)

After scoring the squid in a diamond pattern, cut it into pieces.

Lightly coat the squid in the cornflour mixture, shaking off any excess.

When the squid is golden and curled up, remove from the oil with a slotted spoon.

THAI FISH CAKES

Preparation time: 20 minutes
Total cooking time: 20 minutes
Serves 4–6

500 g (1 lb 2 oz) redfish fillets,
   chopped
1 stem lemon grass, white part
   only, chopped
2 tablespoons fish sauce
5 spring onions (scallions), chopped
3 tablespoons chopped coriander
   (cilantro)
1 clove garlic, crushed
140 ml (5 fl oz) can coconut milk
1 tablespoon sweet chilli sauce
1 egg
5 snake beans, finely sliced
oil, for shallow-frying
200 g (7 oz) mixed lettuce leaves

Sauce
90 g (1/3 cup) sugar
2 tablespoons sweet chilli sauce
1/2 small Lebanese (short) cucumber,
   diced

1 Place the fish, lemon grass, fish sauce, spring onion, coriander, garlic, coconut milk, sweet chilli sauce and egg in a food processor or blender and blend until smooth. Transfer to a bowl and fold in the snake beans. With wet hands, shape into twelve 7 cm (2¾ inch) fish cakes, about 1 cm (¾ inch) high. Place on a plate, then cover and refrigerate.
2 For the sauce, stir the sugar and 80 ml (1/3 cup) water in a small saucepan over low heat for 2 minutes, or until all the sugar has dissolved. Increase the heat and simmer for 5 minutes, or until slightly thickened. Remove from the heat and stir in the

sweet chilli sauce. Cool and stir in the diced cucumber.
3 Heat the oil in a large, deep, heavy-based frying pan and cook the fish cakes in batches over medium heat for 1–2 minutes on each side, or until cooked through.

4 Divide the lettuce among the plates and arrange the fish cakes on top. Serve with the sauce.

NUTRITION PER SERVE (6)
Protein 21 g; Fat 11 g; Carbohydrate 19 g; Dietary Fibre 1.5 g; Cholesterol 88.5 mg; 1055 kJ (250 cal)

Using wet hands, shape the mixture into 12 patties.

Remove from the heat and stir the sweet chilli sauce into the sugar syrup.

Cook the fish cakes on both sides, turning with a spatula, until cooked through.

FRIED WHITEBAIT

Preparation time: 10 minutes
Total cooking time: 5 minutes
Serves 6

750 g (1 lb 10 oz) whitebait
185 g (1½ cups) plain (all-purpose)
    flour
4 tablespoons ready-made
    Moroccan spices

1 teaspoon cayenne pepper
oil, for deep-frying
mixed lettuce leaves, for serving
lemon wedges, for serving

1 Rinse the whitebait under cold water, then drain and pat dry with paper towels.
2 Stir the flour in a bowl with the Moroccan spices, cayenne pepper and 1 teaspoon salt. Add the whitebait and toss to coat. Shake off any excess.

3 Fill a wok or deep heavy-based saucepan one third full of oil and heat to 190°C (375°F), or until a cube of bread browns in 10 seconds. Cook the whitebait in batches for 30 seconds, or until golden brown. Drain on paper towels and season with salt. Serve on a bed of lettuce with lemon wedges.

NUTRITION PER SERVE
Protein 30 g; Fat 10.5 g; Carbohydrate 26 g; Dietary Fibre 3.5 g; Cholesterol 87.5 mg; 1330 kJ (315 cal)

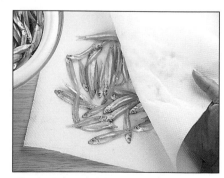

Rinse all the whitebait under cold running water, then drain and pat dry.

Toss the dried whitebait in the flour and spice mixture and shake off any excess.

Deep-fry the coated whitebait in batches for about 30 seconds, until golden brown.

SASHIMI TIMBALES

Preparation time: 25 minutes
  + 15 minutes standing
Total cooking time: 15 minutes
Serves 6

Sushi Rice
440 g (2 cups) short- or
    medium-grain rice
1½ tablespoons sugar
125 ml (½ cup) Japanese
    rice vinegar
2 tablespoons mirin

Wasabi Mayonnaise
250 g (1 cup) whole-egg mayonnaise
2 tablespoons Japanese rice
    vinegar
3 teaspoons wasabi paste

3 sheets nori
300 g (10½ oz) good-quality salmon,
    very thinly sliced
1 avocado
toasted black sesame seeds,
    for serving
pickled ginger, finely sliced,
    for serving
Japanese soy sauce, for serving

1 Rinse the rice under cold water until the water runs clear. Place in a saucepan with 625 ml (2½ cups) water, cover, bring to the boil, then reduce the heat and simmer for 8–10 minutes, or until all the water is absorbed and holes form on top. Remove from the heat and leave, covered, for 15 minutes, or until cooked through.
2 Meanwhile, put the sugar, vinegar, mirin and ½ teaspoon salt in a small saucepan and stir over medium heat for 2–3 minutes, or until the sugar has dissolved. Lay the rice out on a flat

non-metallic tray, pour the vinegar mixture over the top and stir through.
3 For the wasabi mayonnaise, mix all the ingredients together in a bowl.
4 Cut circles from the nori to fit the bases of six 250 ml (1 cup) ramekins. Cover the base of each ramekin with 50 g (1¾ oz) salmon. Spread 2 teaspoons of the wasabi mayonnaise over each salmon layer. Top with nori, then fill each ramekin three-quarters full using about 125 g

(²⁄₃ cup) sushi rice. Refrigerate until just before serving.
5 Cut the avocado into cubes. Dip a knife in hot water and run around the ramekin edges to loosen the rice. Turn out, top with avocado and sprinkle with sesame seeds. Serve with the mayonnaise, ginger and soy sauce.

NUTRITION PER SERVE
Protein 20.5 g; Fat 25.5 g; Carbohydrate 71.5 g; Dietary Fibre 3 g; Cholesterol 37.5 mg; 2495 kJ (595 cal)

Remove from the heat when all the water is absorbed and holes form on top.

Using the ramekins as a guide, cut circles from the nori with a sharp knife.

To release the rice, dip a knife in hot water and run it around the edges.

TUNA PARCELS

Preparation time: 15 minutes
+ 20 minutes standing
Total cooking time: 50 minutes
Serves 6

Pancakes
155 g (1¼ cups) plain (all-purpose)
    flour
45 g (¼ cup) rice flour
2 eggs, lightly beaten
melted butter or oil, for greasing

Filling
1 tablespoon oil
1 onion, finely chopped
2 cloves garlic, crushed
80 g (½ cup) capers
75 g (½ cup) black olives, pitted,
    chopped
1 tomato, diced
250 g (9 oz) English spinach, roughly
    chopped
3 tablespoons chopped flat-leaf
    (Italian) parsley
1 tablespoon lemon juice
185 g (6 oz) can tuna in springwater,
    drained and flaked

2 eggs, lightly beaten
2 teaspoons cornflour (cornstarch)
80 ml (⅓ cup) olive oil

1 Sift the flours into a bowl, make a well and gradually whisk in the eggs and 625 ml (2½ cups) water. Mix to a smooth lump-free batter. Cover and set aside for 20 minutes.

2 Heat a large frying pan and brush lightly with melted butter or oil. Pour 60 ml (¼ cup) batter into the pan and swirl to make a 16–20 cm (6½–8 inch) pancake. Cook over low heat for 1 minute, or until bubbles appear on the surface and the underside is golden. Turn over and cook for 20 seconds. Transfer to a plate and repeat to make 12 pancakes.

3 For the filling, heat the oil in a frying pan, add the onion and garlic and cook over medium heat for 2–3 minutes, or until the onion is soft. Add the capers, olives and tomato and cook, stirring occasionally, for 5–8 minutes, or until the liquid has evaporated. Reduce the heat to low, add the spinach, cover and steam for 2 minutes, or until the leaves wilt.

Remove from the heat and stir in the parsley, lemon juice and tuna. Cool and drain any excess liquid. Season.

4 For the coating, lightly stir the eggs, cornflour and 60 ml (¼ cup) water together in a shallow dish.

5 Lay the pancakes on a work surface. Place 1 tablespoon of filling in the centre of each. Fold into a parcel and secure with a toothpick.

6 Heat the oil in a frying pan over medium heat. Dip the filled pancakes into the egg coating, allowing any excess to drain off. Fry the pancakes in batches for 3 minutes each side, or until golden and heated through. Serve hot.

NUTRITION PER SERVE
Protein 17.5 g; Fat 22.5 g; Carbohydrate 28.5 g; Dietary Fibre 4 g; Cholesterol 140.5 mg; 1610 kJ (385 cal)

COOK'S FILE

VARIATION: Use a can of salmon.

Place a tablespoon of filling in the centre of each pancake, fold over and secure.

Turn the pancakes over and cook until golden and heated through.

BASIL MUSSELS

Preparation time: 25 minutes
Total cooking time: 10 minutes
Serves 6

1 kg (2 lb 4 oz) black mussels
2 teaspoons butter
2 red Asian shallots, chopped
125 ml (1/2 cup) dry white wine

Basil Butter
50 g (1¾ oz) butter
10 g (¼ oz) fresh basil leaves
1 clove garlic, chopped
2 tablespoons dry breadcrumbs

1 Scrub the mussels with a stiff brush and pull out the hairy beards. Discard any broken mussels or open ones that don't close when tapped on the bench. Rinse well.
2 Melt the butter in a large saucepan over medium heat. Add the shallots and cook for 2 minutes, or until soft. Add the wine and mussels, increase the heat and cook for 4–5 minutes, stirring occasionally, until the mussels have opened. Remove the open mussels and discard unopened ones.
3 For the basil butter, process all the ingredients together in a food processor or blender until smooth. Season with ground black pepper.

4 Separate the mussel shells, leaving the meat on one half. Discard the empty shells. Place a teaspoon of basil butter on each mussel. Arrange on a foil-lined griller (broiler) tray and cook under a hot griller (broiler) for 1 minute, or until the butter is melted. Season with salt and black pepper.

NUTRITION PER SERVE
Protein 20.5 g; Fat 12 g; Carbohydrate 8 g; Dietary Fibre 0.5 g; Cholesterol 72.5 mg; 1005 kJ (240 cal)

COOK'S FILE

VARIATION: Use scallops on the half shell—remove hard muscle, continue from step 3 and grill for 2 minutes.

Scrub all the dirt from the mussels with a stiff brush.

Pull the mussel shells apart, leaving the mussel meat on one of the half shells.

Spoon a teaspoon of the basil butter over the meat on each mussel.

CHARGRILLED PRAWNS

Preparation time: 15 minutes
  + 30 minutes marinating
Total cooking time: 5 minutes
Serves 4

8 very large raw prawns (shrimp)
  (about 800 g/1 lb 12 oz)
1 tablespoon sweet chilli sauce
1 teaspoon ground coriander
125 ml (½ cup) olive oil
80 ml (⅓ cup) lime juice
3 cloves garlic, crushed
1 tomato, peeled, seeded and
  chopped

2 tablespoons roughly chopped
  coriander (cilantro)
200 g (7 oz) mixed salad leaves,
  for serving

1 Remove the heads from the prawns and, with a sharp knife, cut the prawns in half lengthways, leaving the tails attached. Pull out each dark vein.
2 Mix the sweet chilli sauce and ground coriander in a large bowl with half the olive oil, half the lime juice and half the garlic. Add the prawns, toss to coat thoroughly, then cover and marinate in the refrigerator for 30 minutes.
3 Meanwhile, to make the dressing, mix the remaining olive oil, lime juice and garlic in a bowl with the chopped tomato and fresh coriander.
4 Heat a barbecue or chargrill plate to hot. Drain the prawns, reserving the marinade, and place cut-side down on the barbecue. Cook, brushing with the marinade, for 1–2 minutes each side, or until cooked through.
5 For serving, divide the mixed salad leaves among the plates and arrange some prawns over the top. Spoon a little of the dressing over the prawns and season with salt and freshly ground black pepper.

NUTRITION PER SERVE
Protein 42 g; Fat 31 g; Carbohydrate 2.5 g;
Dietary Fibre 2 g; Cholesterol 298 mg;
1930 kJ (460 cal)

Cut each prawn through the centre lengthways, leaving the tail attached.

Cook both sides of the drained prawns on a hot chargrill plate or barbecue.

Stir the dressing ingredients together in a bowl until well combined.

CAJUN PRAWN CAKES

Preparation time: 35 minutes
+ 30 minutes refrigeration
Total cooking time: 30 minutes
Makes 24 patties

1 teaspoon oil
6 red Asian shallots, chopped
2 cloves garlic, chopped
2 small red chillies, seeded,
    chopped
1 kg (2 lb 4 oz) raw prawns (shrimp),
    peeled and deveined
2 tablespoons cornflour (cornstarch)
2 egg whites, lightly beaten
100 g (1 cup) dry breadcrumbs
2½ teaspoons Cajun spices
60 ml (¼ cup) oil, extra, for
    shallow-frying

Mustard Sauce
30 g (1 oz) butter
3 spring onions (scallions), finely
    sliced
2 teaspoons plain (all-purpose) flour
80 ml (⅓ cup) cream
1 teaspoon lemon juice
1 tablespoon wholegrain mustard

1 Heat the oil in a frying pan, add the shallots, garlic and chilli and cook over medium heat for 2–3 minutes, or until the shallots soften. Cool.
2 Process the prawns in a food processor with the shallot mixture until combined. Add the cornflour, egg white, 50 g (½ cup) breadcrumbs and 2 teaspoons Cajun spices and process until combined. Transfer to a bowl. Mix the remaining breadcrumbs and Cajun spices in a separate bowl.
3 Using a tablespoon of prawn mixture at a time, shape into 24 small patties and coat in the combined breadcrumbs and spices. Place on a tray and cover with plastic wrap. Refrigerate for 30 minutes.
4 Meanwhile, to make the mustard sauce, melt the butter in a saucepan, add the spring onion and cook over medium heat for 2 minutes, or until softened. Add the flour and stir for 1 minute, or until pale and foaming. Remove from the heat and stir in the cream a little at a time until well combined. Return the saucepan to the heat and stir over low heat for 1 minute, or until thickened. Stir in the lemon juice and mustard.
5 Heat the extra oil in a frying pan and cook the patties in batches over medium heat for 2–3 minutes on each side, or until golden. Drain on paper towels. Serve with the mustard sauce.

NUTRITION PER PATTY
Protein 6.5 g; Fat 6 g; Carbohydrate 7 g;
Dietary Fibre 0.5 g; Cholesterol 67 mg;
375 kJ (90 cal)

Roll the prawn patties in the combined breadcrumbs and spices

Stir the sauce over low heat with a wooden spoon until thickened.

Cook the patties for a couple of minutes on each side until golden.

SUSHI AND SASHIMI

Ingredients for these Japanese delicacies are available from speciality stores. Shoyu is a soy sauce, lighter and sweeter than the Chinese one. Wasabi has a fierce flavour, rather like horseradish, and comes in paste or powder form. Nori is dried seaweed, sold in sheets.

SUSHI RICE

Put 550 g (2½ cups) white short-grain rice in a fine colander and rinse under cold water until the water runs clear. Drain and leave in the colander for 1 hour. Transfer to a large saucepan, add 750 ml (3 cups) water, bring to the boil and cook, without stirring, for 5–10 minutes, or until tunnels form on the surface. Reduce the heat to low, cover and cook for 12–15 minutes, or until tender. Remove from the heat and set aside for 15 minutes. Place 5 tablespoons rice vinegar, 1 tablespoon mirin, 2 teaspoons salt and 2 tablespoons sugar in a bowl and stir until the sugar dissolves. Spread the rice over a flat non-metallic tray and stir the dressing through. Spread out and cool to body temperature. If the rice gets too cold, it will be difficult to work with. Cover with a damp tea towel. To prevent the rice sticking to your hands, dip your fingers in a bowl of warm water with a few drops of rice vinegar added. Makes 1.2 kg (6 cups).

SALMON AND CUCUMBER ROLLS

Cut a 200 g (7 oz) fillet of sashimi salmon on an angle into paper-thin slices. Cut 1 Lebanese (short) cucumber in half lengthways and scoop out the seeds. Halve widthways and cut into thin strips. Place the salmon on a board, top each slice with a few cucumber strips, roll up and tie with chives. Serve with ginger, shoyu and wasabi. Makes about 24.

CALIFORNIA ROLLS

Place 1 sheet of nori on a bamboo mat, shiny-side-down. Spread 150 g (¾ cup) cooked sushi rice in the middle of the sheet, leaving a 2 cm (¾ inch) border along the end nearest you. Make a slight indentation along the centre of the rice to hold the filling, then spread a small line of Japanese mayonnaise along the ridge. Spread about 1 tablespoon flying fish roe over the mayonnaise and top with 2 or 3 cooked, peeled, deveined, halved prawns (shrimp) or chopped crab stick. Roll the mat over to enclose the filling, then roll, pressing to form a firm roll. Slice into 6. Repeat, using the same quantities, to make 3 more rolls. You will need 600 g (3 cups) cooked sushi rice altogether. Makes 24.

SASHIMI

With a sharp broad knife, remove any skin from 500 g (1 lb 2 oz) good-quality, very fresh fish such as tuna, salmon or kingfish. Freeze until firm enough to cut into slices about 5 mm (¼ inch) thick. Make each cut in one motion, in one direction. Arrange on a serving platter and serve with wasabi and shoyu. Serves 4–6.

PRAWN AND TUNA NIGIRI

Peel and butterfly 10 cooked prawns (shrimp). Trim 250 g (9 oz) good-quality tuna into a rectangle, removing any connective tissue or blood, then cut into thin slices, wiping the knife after each slice. Form a tablespoon of sushi rice into an oval the same length and width as the fish. Place one tuna slice flat on your hand, then spread a dab of wasabi paste over the centre. Place the rice on the fish and cup your palm. Press the rice onto the fish, firmly pushing with a slight upward motion to make a neat shape. Turn over and repeat the shaping process, finishing with the fish on top. Repeat until you have used all the tuna and the prawns. You will need 400 g (2 cups) cooked sushi rice. Makes 16–20.

INSIDE-OUT ROLLS

Place a nori sheet on a bamboo mat and spread 1 cm (½ inch) cooked sushi rice over the top, leaving a 1 cm (½ inch) border at one end. Cover with a sheet of plastic wrap larger than the nori. In one quick motion, turn the whole thing over, then place it back on the mat, so the plastic is under the rice and the nori on top. Spread a little wasabi paste on the nori, along the short end, 4 cm (1½ inches) from the edge. Lay thin strips of Lebanese (short) cucumber, thin strips of avocado and about 25 g (1 oz) fresh crab meat on top of the wasabi, then roll from this end, using the plastic as a guide. Wrap in plastic, then roll up in the mat, to form a firm roll. Unroll and discard the plastic. Roll in flying fish roe, or toasted black sesame seeds. Using a very sharp knife, trim the ends, then cut into six. Repeat to make another 7 rolls. You will need 1.2 kg (6 cups) cooked sushi rice and 200 g (7 oz) crab meat altogether. Serve with shoyu. Makes 48.

TUNA/SALMON NORI ROLLS

Cut 5 sheets of nori in half lengthways. Cut 200 g (7 oz) sashimi tuna or salmon into thin strips. Place a piece of nori on a bamboo mat, shiny-side down, and spread 4 tablespoons cooked sushi rice over it, leaving a 2 cm (¾ inch) border along one end. Make a slight indentation along the centre, then dab a small amount of wasabi paste along the ridge. Top with fish. Roll the mat to enclose the filling, pressing to form a firm roll. Slice the roll into six pieces. Repeat to use all the nori pieces and fish. You will need 800 g (4 cups) cooked sushi rice altogether. Makes 60.

Clockwise, from top left: Inside-out rolls; California rolls; Sashimi; Salmon and cucumber rolls; Tuna/salmon nori rolls; Prawn and tuna nigiri.

SALMON CARPACCIO

Preparation time: 30 minutes
+ 30 minutes freezing
Total cooking time: Nil
Serves 4

500 g (1 lb 2 oz) good-quality salmon
3 vine-ripened tomatoes
1 tablespoon baby capers, well
    rinsed and drained
1 tablespoon chopped dill
1 tablespoon extra virgin
    olive oil
1 tablespoon lime juice
ciabatta bread, for serving

1 Wrap the salmon piece in foil and freeze for 20–30 minutes, or until partly frozen.

2 Meanwhile, cut a cross in the base of each tomato, place in a bowl and pour in enough boiling water to cover. Stand for 2–3 minutes, until the skin softens, then drain and peel. Cut each tomato in half, scoop out the seeds with a teaspoon and dice the flesh. Place in a bowl and stir in the capers and dill.

3 Remove the salmon from the freezer and unwrap. Using a very sharp knife, carefully cut the salmon into thin slices, cutting across the grain. Divide the salmon equally among four plates, arranging in a single layer, or use a serving platter.

4 Whisk together the olive oil and lime juice in a small bowl and season with a large pinch of salt or sea salt. Drizzle this dressing over the salmon just before serving. Season with freshly ground black pepper and serve immediately with the tomato mixture and slices of ciabatta bread.

NUTRITION PER SERVE
Protein 36.5 g; Fat 12 g; Carbohydrate 32.5 g; Dietary Fibre 3 g; Cholesterol 60 mg; 1635 kJ (390 cal)

COOK'S FILE

NOTE: For this recipe, you can also use very fresh, good-quality tuna or smoked salmon. If you don't have a lot of time, the salmon can be thinly sliced without partially freezing it—use a very sharp knife.

VARIATION: You can add a small amount of finely grated lime or lemon zest to the tomato mixture.

Cut the peeled tomatoes in half and scoop out the seeds with a teaspoon.

Freezing the salmon makes it easier to cut into very thin slices.

SALMON RAVIOLI WITH CREAMY SAUCE

Preparation time: 30 minutes
Total cooking time: 25 minutes
Serves 6

1 tablespoon olive oil
1 small leek, finely sliced
2 cloves garlic, crushed
½ teaspoon finely grated lime zest
400 g (14 oz) salmon fillet, skin and
    bones removed, diced
1 tablespoon chopped dill
1 teaspoon lime juice
1 egg white, lightly beaten
60 gow gee wrappers

50 g (1¾ oz) butter
4 spring onions (scallions), sliced
    diagonally
2 cloves garlic, crushed, extra
300 ml (10½ fl oz) cream

1 Heat the oil in a frying pan over medium heat, add the leek and garlic and cook for 1–2 minutes, or until soft. Transfer to a food processor and add the lime zest, salmon, dill, lime juice, egg white, salt and ground black pepper. Process until just combined.
2 Lay 30 gow gee wrappers on a work surface and brush the edges with water. Top each with 1 heaped teaspoon of salmon mixture, then cover each with a wrapper, pressing the edges together. Place on a tray and cover with a tea towel.
3 Melt the butter in a frying pan. Add the spring onion and extra garlic and cook for 1 minute. Stir in the cream, bring to the boil, then reduce the heat and simmer for 4–5 minutes, or until the cream has reduced and slightly thickened. Keep warm.
4 Bring a large saucepan of salted water to the boil. Cook batches of the ravioli for 2–4 minutes, or until the pasta is tender. Drain. Divide among serving plates and top with the sauce.

NUTRITION PER SERVE
Protein 18.5 g; Fat 34.5 g; Carbohydrate 8.5 g; Dietary Fibre 1 g; Cholesterol 122 mg; 1740 kJ (415 cal)

Put filling on 30 wrappers, cover each with a wrapper and press the edges.

Stir the sauce with a wooden spoon until reduced and slightly thickened.

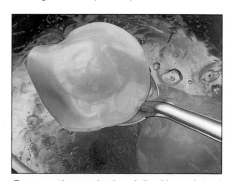

Remove the cooked ravioli with a slotted spoon and drain.

SCALLOPS WITH PASTA

Preparation time: 10 minutes
Total cooking time: 20 minutes
Serves 4

20 large scallops, without roe
250 g (9 oz) dried linguini
150 ml (5½ fl oz) extra virgin olive oil
2 cloves garlic, finely chopped
½ teaspoon dried chilli flakes
60 ml (¼ cup) white wine
1 tablespoon lemon juice
100 g (3½ oz) baby rocket (arugula)
    leaves

6 tablespoons chopped coriander
    (cilantro)

1 Slice or pull off any membrane or hard muscle from the scallops and pat the scallops dry with paper towel.
2 Cook the linguini in a large saucepan of rapidly boiling salted water for 12 minutes, or until *al dente*.
3 Heat 1 tablespoon of the oil in a frying pan, add the garlic and stir for a few seconds (don't brown). Stir in the chilli flakes, wine and lemon juice, then remove from heat.
4 Drain the pasta, put in a bowl and toss with 1 tablespoon of the oil. Heat

a barbecue or chargrill plate over high heat and brush with a little oil. Season the scallops and cook for 1 minute each side, or until just cooked.
5 Heat the garlic and chilli mixture gently, add the baby rocket leaves and stir over medium heat until wilted. Toss through the pasta, then toss with the remaining olive oil and half the coriander. Serve mounds of pasta with scallops on top. Garnish with the remaining coriander.

NUTRITION PER SERVE
Protein 16 g; Fat 37 g; Carbohydrate 45 g; Dietary Fibre 4 g; Cholesterol 23.5 mg; 2445 kJ (580 cal)

Toss the drained pasta with 1 tablespoon of the oil.

Cook the seasoned scallops on an oiled, heated barbecue or chargrill plate.

Wilt the baby rocket leaves in a pan with the heated garlic and chilli mixture.

PARMESAN PRAWNS

Preparation time: 30 minutes
  + 15 minutes refrigeration
Total cooking time: 10 minutes
Serves 6

1 kg (2 lb 4 oz) raw king prawns
    (shrimp)
125 g (1 cup) plain (all-purpose) flour
2 eggs, lightly beaten
150 g (1½ cups) dry breadcrumbs
50 g (½ cup) grated Parmesan cheese
1 tablespoon finely chopped flat-leaf
    (Italian) parsley
light olive oil, for deep-frying
100 g (3½ oz) mixed salad greens

Tomato Salsa
1 tablespoon extra virgin olive oil
1 tablespoon lime juice
2 cloves garlic, crushed
3 small Roma (plum) tomatoes,
    peeled, seeded and finely diced
10 black olives, pitted, chopped
1 tablespoon finely shredded basil
1 tablespoon capers, finely chopped
2 tablespoons whole-egg mayonnaise

1 Peel the prawns, leaving the tails intact. Gently pull out the dark vein from each prawn back, starting at the head end.
2 Measure the flour into a bowl and put the eggs in a separate bowl. Mix the breadcrumbs, Parmesan, parsley and salt and pepper, to taste, in another bowl.
3 Season the flour and add the prawns, in batches, and lightly toss to coat, shaking off any excess. Dip into the egg, then roll in the breadcrumbs, pressing the crumbs on firmly. Place on a tray and refrigerate, uncovered, for 15 minutes.

4 For the salsa, whisk the oil, lime juice and garlic together in a bowl until combined. Stir in the tomato, olives, basil, capers, mayonnaise, and salt and pepper, to taste.
5 Fill a deep saucepan one third full of oil and heat to 180°C (350°F), or until a cube of bread dropped in the oil browns in 15 seconds. Deep-fry batches of prawns for 1–2 minutes, or

until golden. Drain on crumpled paper towels.
6 For serving, arrange the prawns over some of the salad greens. Season with salt and pepper, to taste. Serve with the tomato salsa.

NUTRITION PER SERVE
Protein 46 g; Fat 15 g; Carbohydrate 34.5 g; Dietary Fibre 3.5 g; Cholesterol 318.5 mg; 1930 kJ (460 cal)

Toss the prawns in flour, dip in the egg, then press firmly in the breadcrumbs.

Mix the oil, juice and garlic, then stir in the remaining salsa ingredients.

When the prawns are golden and cooked through, remove with a slotted spoon.

SALMON CAKES WITH HERB MAYONNAISE

Preparation time: 20 minutes
Total cooking time: 20 minutes
Makes 36

500 g (1 lb 2 oz) salmon fillet, skin
    and bones removed, cut into
    5 mm (⅛ inch) cubes
3 tablespoons dry breadcrumbs
1 tablespoon lightly beaten egg
½ teaspoon finely grated
    lime zest
3½ teaspoons lime juice
3 teaspoons dill, chopped
125 g (½ cup) whole-egg
    mayonnaise
1 clove garlic, crushed
2 tablespoons light olive oil

1 Place the salmon, breadcrumbs, egg, lime zest, 3 teaspoons lime juice and 2 teaspoons dill in a bowl. Stir until the mixture comes together and the ingredients are evenly distributed. Season well with salt and freshly ground black pepper.

2 With wet hands, using 2 heaped teaspoons of mixture at a time, shape into 36 small round cakes. Place on a baking tray lined with baking paper. Refrigerate until ready to use.

3 For the herb mayonnaise, mix the remaining lime juice and dill with the mayonnaise and garlic in a bowl.

4 Heat the olive oil in a large non-stick frying pan. Cook the salmon cakes in batches over medium heat for 2 minutes each side, or until golden and cooked through. Do not overcook. Drain on paper towels. Top each with a little of the herb mayonnaise and season well. Serve immediately. Looks attractive with strips of lime zest.

NUTRITION PER CAKE
Protein 3.5 g; Fat 3 g; Carbohydrate 1 g; Dietary Fibre 0 g; Cholesterol 13 mg; 195 kJ (45 cal)

COOK'S FILE

VARIATION: You can also top these with 125 ml (½ cup) crème fraîche and 1½ tablespoons salmon roe.

Use a clean set of tweezers to remove any bones from the salmon.

Use 2 teaspoons of mixture for each cake, shaping with wet hands.

After 2 minutes, turn the salmon cakes over and cook until golden.

SWEET CITRUS SCALLOP SALAD

Preparation time: 20 minutes
Total cooking time: 20 minutes
Serves 4

Lemon and Herb Dressing
½ preserved lemon
60 ml (¼ cup) olive oil
2 tablespoons lemon juice
1 tablespoon sweet chilli sauce
2 tablespoons white wine
     vinegar
2 tablespoons chopped coriander
     (cilantro)

500 g (1 lb 2 oz) potatoes
oil, for shallow-frying
750 g (1 lb 10 oz) scallops, without roe
2 tablespoons olive oil, extra
75 g (2½ oz) baby English spinach
     leaves

1 For the dressing, scoop out and discard the pulp from the preserved lemon, wash the skin and cut into thin slices. Put in a bowl and whisk with the olive oil, lemon juice, sweet chilli sauce, wine vinegar and coriander.
2 Cut the potatoes into paper-thin slices. Heat 2 cm (¾ inch) oil in a deep heavy-based frying pan and cook batches of the potato for 1–2 minutes,

or until crisp and golden. Drain on crumpled paper towels.
3 Slice or pull off any membrane, vein or hard white muscle from the scallops. Heat the extra oil in a frying pan over high heat and cook batches of scallops for 1–2 minutes, or until golden brown on both sides.
4 Divide half the spinach among four plates. Top with potato, then half the scallops and more spinach. Finish with more scallops. Drizzle with the dressing just before serving.

NUTRITION PER SERVE
Protein 25.5 g; Fat 30.5 g; Carbohydrate 20 g; Dietary Fibre 3.5 g; Cholesterol 62 mg; 1890 kJ (450 cal)

Use a spoon to scoop out the pulpy centre from the preserved lemon.

Remove the crisp golden potato crisps from the oil with a slotted spoon.

Cook batches of scallops until golden on both sides.

GARLIC PRAWNS

Preparation time: 20 minutes
Total cooking time: 15 minutes
Serves 4

1.25 kg (2 lb 12 oz) raw medium
    prawns (shrimp)
80 g (2½ oz) butter, melted
185 ml (¾ cup) olive oil
8 cloves garlic, crushed
2 spring onions (scallions), thinly sliced

1 Preheat the oven to 250°C (500°F/ Gas 10). Peel the prawns, leaving the tails intact. Gently pull out the dark vein from each prawn back, starting at the head end. Cut a slit down the back of each prawn.
2 Combine the butter and oil and divide among four 500 ml (2 cup) cast iron pots. Divide half the crushed garlic among the pots.
3 Place the pots on a baking tray in the oven for 10 minutes, or until bubbling. Divide the prawns and remaining garlic among the pots. Return to the oven for 5 minutes, or until the prawns are cooked. Stir in the spring onion. Season, to taste. Serve with crusty bread.

NUTRITION PER SERVE
Protein 20 g; Fat 61 g; Carbohydrate 1 g; Dietary Fibre 1 g; Cholesterol 192.5 mg; 2620 kJ (625 cal)

COOK'S FILE

NOTE: Garlic prawns can also be made in a cast iron frying pan in the oven.

Carefully cut a slit down the back of each prawn with a sharp knife.

When the mixture in the pots is bubbling, remove from the oven.

Divide the prawns and remaining crushed garlic among the pots.

PENNE WITH PRAWNS

Preparation time: 30 minutes
Total cooking time: 45 minutes
Serves 4

3 Roma (plum) tomatoes
375 g (13 oz) penne
500 g (1 lb 2 oz) cooked medium
  prawns (shrimp)
100 g (3½ oz) baby English spinach
  leaves
125 g (4½ oz) goats cheese,
  crumbled
40 g (¼ cup) pine nuts, toasted

Garlic Dressing
2 cloves garlic, crushed
60 ml (¼ cup) extra virgin olive oil
2 teaspoons finely grated lemon zest
2 tablespoons lemon juice
1 tablespoon chopped flat-leaf
  (Italian) parsley

1 Preheat the oven to 180°C (350°F/ Gas 4). Cut each Roma tomato lengthways into 6 wedges and bake on a baking tray lined with baking paper for 45 minutes, or until the wedges are just starting to dry out around the edges. Remove and cool.
2 Cook the penne in a large saucepan of rapidly boiling salted water for 12 minutes, or until *al dente*. Drain and cool. Transfer to a large bowl.
3 Meanwhile, peel the prawns, leaving the tails intact. Gently pull out the dark vein from each prawn back, starting at the head end.

4 Add the cooled tomato, prawns, spinach and cheese to the pasta and toss well.
5 For the garlic dressing, place all the ingredients in a screw top jar, screw the lid on tightly and shake well. Pour over the salad and toss until well distributed. Sprinkle with pine nuts and serve.

NUTRITION PER SERVE
Protein 48.5 g; Fat 31 g; Carbohydrate 68.5 g; Dietary Fibre 7 g; Cholesterol 256.5 mg; 3135 kJ (750 cal)

Bake the tomato wedges until just starting to dry out around the edges.

Toss the prawns, tomato, spinach and cheese with the cooled pasta.

SALADS

SALAD NICOISE WITH SEARED TUNA

Preparation time: 10 minutes
Total cooking time: 20 minutes
Serves 4

12 baby new or small chat potatoes, or 250 g (9 oz) kipfler potatoes
150 g (5½ oz) small green beans
2 x 200 g (7 oz) tuna fillets
2 tablespoons olive oil
180 g (6 oz) mixed lettuce leaves
2 ripe tomatoes, cut into wedges
60 g (½ cup) small black olives
4 hard-boiled eggs, quartered

Dressing
2 tablespoons lemon juice
60 ml (¼ cup) extra virgin olive oil
1 teaspoon Dijon mustard

1 Steam the whole potatoes in a steamer for 10 minutes, or until just tender (pierce with the point of a small sharp knife—if the potato comes away easily, it is ready). Drain thoroughly and keep warm.
2 Trim the beans and steam for 2 minutes. Drain and keep warm.
3 Brush the tuna fillets with oil and sprinkle both sides generously with freshly ground black pepper. Heat a barbecue or chargrill plate over high heat and brush with oil. Add the tuna and cook for 1–2 minutes on one side. Turn it over and cook the other side until seared on the outside. The tuna should still be pink in the centre. Remove the tuna, cool slightly, then cut into bite-sized cubes.
4 For the dressing, thoroughly whisk together the juice, oil and mustard in a large bowl. Season well.
5 To assemble the salad, divide the lettuce leaves among four serving plates. Cut the potatoes in half (if using kipfler, cut into thick slices). Put the potatoes, beans, tuna, tomatoes and olives in the dressing and toss gently. Spoon over the lettuce. Season well with salt and freshly ground black pepper and top with the egg quarters.

NUTRITION PER SERVE
Protein 33.5 g; Fat 35 g; Carbohydrate 12 g; Dietary Fibre 4.5 g; Cholesterol 244 mg; 2095 kJ (500 cal)

COOK'S FILE

ALTERNATIVE FISH: Fresh salmon, canned tuna.
NOTE: Chat potatoes are small washed potatoes.
VARIATION: You can add chopped anchovies, capers and parsley to the dressing. If you find the flavour of anchovies too strong, chop them in a processor with all the dressing ingredients until smooth, then stir through as above.

Don't overcook the tuna. Just sear the outside—the centre should still be pink.

When cooled, cut the seared tuna into bite-sized cubes.

SMOKED SALMON AND ROCKET SALAD

Preparation time: 20 minutes
Total cooking time: Nil
Serves 4

Dressing
1 tablespoon extra virgin
    olive oil
2 tablespoons balsamic vinegar

150 g (5½ oz) rocket (arugula) leaves
1 avocado
250 g (9 oz) smoked salmon
325 g (11½ oz) jar marinated goats
    cheese, drained and crumbled
2 tablespoons roasted hazelnuts,
    coarsely chopped

1 For the dressing, thoroughly whisk together the oil and vinegar in a bowl. Season, to taste. Trim long stems from the rocket, rinse, pat dry and gently toss in a bowl with the dressing.
2 Cut the avocado in half lengthways, then cut each half lengthways into 6 wedges. Discard the skin and place 3 wedges on each serving plate and arrange a pile of rocket over the top.
3 Drape pieces of salmon over the rocket. Scatter the cheese and nuts over the top and season with ground black pepper. Serve immediately.

NUTRITION PER SERVE
Protein 31.5 g; Fat 40.5 g; Carbohydrate 1.5 g; Dietary Fibre 2 g; Cholesterol 67.5 mg; 2065 kJ (490 cal)

COOK'S FILE

SUGGESTED FISH: A whole smoked trout can be used instead of the salmon. Peel, remove the bones, then break the flesh into bite-sized pieces.

Drain the goats cheese and crumble into smallish pieces.

Toss the rocket with the dressing in a bowl until well coated.

Cut each avocado half lengthways into six wedges.

PRAWN NOODLE SALAD

Preparation time: 25 minutes
Total cooking time: 5 minutes
Serves 4

125 g (4½ oz) snowpeas (mangetout)
750 g (1 lb 10 oz) medium raw prawns
    (shrimp), peeled and deveined
375 g (13 oz) thin fresh egg noodles
150 g (5½ oz) bean sprouts
4 spring onions (scallions), finely sliced
1 red capsicum (pepper), diced
5 tablespoons chopped coriander
    (cilantro)

Dressing
60 ml (¼ cup) sesame oil
80 ml (⅓ cup) red wine vinegar
80 ml (⅓ cup) kecap manis
2 tablespoons soy sauce

1 Trim the snowpeas and cook them in a small saucepan of boiling water for 1 minute, then transfer to a bowl of iced water. When cold, drain and cut any large ones in half.
2 Cook the prawns in a large saucepan of boiling water for 1–2 minutes, or until the prawns turn pink and are cooked through. Drain and cool, but do not refrigerate.

3 Cook the noodles in a large saucepan of rapidly boiling salted water for 1 minute, or until tender. Drain and leave to cool.
4 For the dressing, thoroughly whisk the ingredients together in a small bowl or jug.
5 Put the snowpeas, prawns, noodles, bean sprouts, spring onion, capsicum and coriander in a large bowl. Add the dressing, toss gently and serve immediately.

NUTRITION PER SERVE
Protein 34.5 g; Fat 16 g; Carbohydrate 28 g; Dietary Fibre 3.5 g; Cholesterol 186.5 mg; 1660 kJ (395 cal)

When the prawns are cooked, remove from the water with a slotted spoon.

Test the noodles after 1 minute to see if they are tender. Don't overcook.

Whisk the dressing ingredients together in a small bowl or jug.

ITALIAN-STYLE PRAWN AND PASTA SALAD

Preparation time: 15 minutes
Total cooking time: 12 minutes
Serves 4

Dressing
80 ml (⅓ cup) olive oil
1½ tablespoons white wine vinegar
1½ tablespoons pine nuts, toasted
1 tablespoon roughly chopped basil
1 tablespoon roughly chopped
    flat-leaf (Italian) parsley
1 clove garlic
1 tablespoon grated Parmesan
pinch of sugar

400 g (14 oz) large pasta shells
1 tablespoon olive oil, extra
500 g (1 lb 2 oz) small cooked
    prawns (shrimp)
100 g (3½ oz) bocconcini, thinly
    sliced
125 g (4½ oz) chargrilled (griddled)
    red capsicum (pepper), cut into
    thin strips
125 g (4½ oz) cherry tomatoes,
    cut in halves
basil leaves, extra, to garnish

1 For the dressing, put the oil, vinegar, pine nuts, basil, parsley, garlic, Parmesan and sugar in a blender or food processor and process together until smooth.

2 Cook the pasta shells in a large saucepan of rapidly boiling salted water for 12 minutes, or until *al dente*. Drain in a colander, then rinse under cold water briefly. Drain thoroughly, return to the saucepan and toss with the extra olive oil. Allow to cool.

3 Peel the prawns and gently pull out the dark vein from each prawn back, starting at the head end.

4 Put the pasta, prawns, bocconcini, capsicum and tomatoes in a serving bowl and pour on the dressing. Toss and garnish with basil leaves.

NUTRITION PER SERVE
Protein 51 g; Fat 35 g; Carbohydrate 73 g; Dietary Fibre 6.5 g; Cholesterol 256.5 mg; 3420 kJ (815 cal)

Cut the chargrilled red capsicum into very thin strips.

Process all the dressing ingredients together until well blended and smooth.

Gently pull out the dark vein from the back of each peeled prawn.

SMOKED TUNA AND WHITE BEAN SALAD WITH BASIL DRESSING

Preparation time: 15 minutes
Total cooking time: Nil
Serves 4

100 g (3½ oz) rocket (arugula)
1 small red capsicum (pepper),
    cut in julienne strips
1 small red onion, chopped
310 g (10½ oz) can cannellini beans
    or white beans, drained
    and rinsed
125 g (4½ oz) cherry tomatoes, cut
    in halves

2 tablespoons capers
2 x 125 g (4½ oz) cans smoked tuna
    slices in oil, drained

Basil Dressing
1 tablespoon lemon juice
1 tablespoon white wine
60 ml (¼ cup) extra virgin
    olive oil
1 clove garlic, crushed
2 teaspoons chopped basil
½ teaspoon sugar

1 Trim any long stems from the rocket, rinse, pat dry and divide among four serving plates.
2 Lightly toss the capsicum in a large bowl with the onion, beans, tomatoes and capers. Spoon some onto each plate, over the rocket, then scatter tuna over each.
3 For the dressing, thoroughly whisk all the ingredients in a bowl with 1 tablespoon of water, ¼ teaspoon of salt and freshly ground or cracked black pepper, to taste. Drizzle over the salad and serve with bread.

NUTRITION PER SERVE
Protein 16 g; Fat 21 g; Carbohydrate 10 g;
Dietary Fibre 5.5 g; Cholesterol 18 mg;
1230 kJ (295 cal)

COOK'S FILE

ALTERNATIVE FISH: Fresh tuna, seared on both sides, then sliced, or canned salmon or tuna.

Cut the red capsicum lengthways into julienne strips.

Use two wooden spoons to toss the capsicum with the other ingredients.

Add the water, salt and pepper to the dressing ingredients and whisk well.

CRAB, MANGO AND PASTA SALAD

Preparation time: 15 minutes
Total cooking time: 12 minutes
Serves 4

150 g (5½ oz) rocket (arugula)
125 g (4½ oz) dried saffron fettucine
125 g (4½ oz) dried squid ink
    fettucine
1 mango, cut into thin strips
1 avocado, sliced
1 red onion, cut into thin wedges

500 g (1 lb 2 oz) fresh or frozen
    crab meat

Dressing
60 ml (¼ cup) olive oil
1 tablespoon whole-egg mayonnaise
2 tablespoons lime juice
1 clove garlic, crushed
¼ teaspoon lime oil or grated lime zest

1 Trim any long stems from the rocket, rinse and dry. Cook the fettucine in a saucepan of rapidly boiling salted water for 12 minutes, or until *al dente*. Drain, cool, then return to the saucepan.

2 For the dressing, combine all the ingredients together in a bowl and whisk thoroughly. Toss through the cooled fettucine.

3 Arrange nests of the fettucine on each serving plate, then top each with some rocket, mango, avocado, red onion and crab meat. Season with salt and freshly ground black pepper, to taste. Delicious served with slices of crusty bread.

NUTRITION PER SERVE
Protein 24.5 g; Fat 26.5 g; Carbohydrate 50 g; Dietary Fibre 5.5 g; Cholesterol 107 mg; 2255 kJ (540 cal)

With a sharp knife, cut the mango flesh into thin strips.

Pull off any long stems from the rocket, then rinse the leaves and pat dry.

When the fettucine has cooled, toss the dressing through until well coated.

MUSSEL SALAD WITH SAFFRON DRESSING

Preparation time: 40 minutes
Total cooking time: 30 minutes
Serves 4–6

750 g (1 lb 10 oz) baby new
    potatoes, unpeeled
1.5 kg (3 lb 5 oz) black mussels
170 ml (⅔ cup) dry white wine
1 small onion, sliced
2 sprigs thyme
2 bay leaves
large pinch saffron threads
125 g (½ cup) sour cream
1 tablespoon finely chopped flat-leaf
    (Italian) parsley

1 Place the potatoes in a saucepan of cold, lightly salted water. Bring to the boil, then reduce the heat and simmer for 15–20 minutes, or until tender. (When pierced with the point of a small knife, the potato will come away easily.) Drain and leave to cool. If you couldn't get baby potatoes, cut large potatoes into quarters or halves.

2 Scrub the mussels with a stiff brush and pull out the hairy beards. Discard any broken mussels, or open ones that don't close when tapped on the bench. Rinse thoroughly. Place the wine, onion, thyme sprigs, bay leaves and half the mussels in a saucepan with a tight-fitting lid. Cover and cook over high heat, stirring once, for about 4–5 minutes, or until the mussels start to open. Remove the mussels as they open, using tongs. Discard any unopened mussels. Cook the remaining mussels the same way, and leave to cool.

3 Strain the mussel cooking liquid and reserve 80 ml (⅓ cup). While still warm, stir in the saffron. Cool, then gradually whisk the mussel liquid into the sour cream and season well with salt and cracked pepper. Stir in the chopped parsley.

4 Remove the flesh from the mussels and discard the shells. Put the mussels and potatoes in a bowl, add the dressing and toss gently to coat.

NUTRITION PER SERVE (6)
Protein 18.5 g; Fat 11.3 g; Carbohydrate 23 g; Dietary Fibre 2.5 g; Cholesterol 62.5 mg; 1235 kJ (292 cal)

Gradually whisk the mussel liquid into the sour cream until smooth.

Gently toss the saffron dressing through the mussels and potatoes.

LAYERED SEAFOOD SALAD

Preparation time: 45 minutes
Total cooking time: 15 minutes
Serves 6

1 kg (2 lb 4 oz) black mussels
24 scallops, with roe
125 ml (½ cup) white wine
500 g (1 lb 2 oz) skinless salmon or
    trout fillets
24 cooked king prawns (shrimp),
    peeled and deveined
150 g (5½ oz) mixed lettuce leaves
1 Lebanese (short) cucumber, sliced

Vinaigrette
60 ml (¼ cup) light olive oil
1 tablespoon white wine vinegar
1 tablespoon lemon juice
1–2 teaspoons sugar
1 teaspoon Dijon mustard

Creamy Herb Dressing
2 egg yolks
2 teaspoons Dijon mustard
2 tablespoons lemon juice
250 ml (1 cup) olive oil
4 anchovy fillets, chopped
1 clove garlic, crushed
60 g (¼ cup) sour cream
3 tablespoons chopped mixed herbs
    (e.g. parsley, dill)

1 Scrub the mussels with a stiff brush and pull out the beards. Discard any broken mussels, or open ones that don't close when tapped. Rinse well. Pull or slice off any vein, membrane or hard white muscle from the scallops. Put 250 ml (1 cup) water in a large saucepan, add the wine and bring to the boil. Add the mussels, cover and steam for 4–5 minutes or until open. Remove with a slotted spoon. Discard any unopened ones. Remove the meat from the shells.

2 Add the scallops to the liquid and poach for 1–2 minutes, or until they just turn white, then remove. Add the fish to the liquid and poach for 4–5 minutes, or until just cooked. Remove and break into large pieces.

3 For the vinaigrette, put the ingredients in a screw top jar, season, tighten the lid and shake. Place all the seafood in a large bowl, add the vinaigrette and toss gently to coat.

4 For the creamy herb dressing, process the egg yolks, mustard and lemon juice in a food processor or blender for 30 seconds, or until light and creamy. With the motor running add the oil in a thin stream and process until thickened. Add the remaining ingredients and pulse for 30 seconds, or until combined.

5 Place half the lettuce and cucumber in a 2.25 litre (9 cup) glass serving bowl. Arrange half the seafood over

Pull the shells apart and remove the mussel meat. Discard unopened mussels.

the greens, then drizzle with half the dressing. Repeat with another layer of greens, seafood and dressing. Serve immediately with crusty bread.

NUTRITION PER SERVE
Protein 55.5 g; Fat 62 g; Carbohydrate 6.5 g; Dietary Fibre 1 g; Cholesterol 282.5 mg; 3425 kJ (820 cal)

COOK'S FILE

ALTERNATIVE FISH: Swordfish, deep-sea perch.

Layer the lettuce and cucumber, seafood and dressing in a serving bowl.

WARM PASTA SALAD

Preparation time: 15 minutes
Total cooking time: 20 minutes
Serves 4

Pesto
2 cloves garlic, crushed
1 teaspoon salt
40 g (¼ cup) pine nuts, toasted
60 g (2 cups) loosely packed basil
50 g (½ cup) grated Parmesan
60 ml (¼ cup) extra virgin olive oil

500 g (1 lb 2 oz) orecchiette pasta
150 g (5½ oz) jar capers in brine,
    drained
3 tablespoons olive oil
2 tablespoons extra virgin olive oil
2 cloves garlic, chopped
2 tomatoes, seeded and diced
155 g (5½ oz) thin asparagus,
    trimmed, cut in halves and
    blanched
2 tablespoons balsamic vinegar
150 g (5½ oz) rocket (arugula),
    trimmed
20 cooked medium prawns (shrimp),
    peeled, tails intact
shaved Parmesan, optional,
    to garnish

1 For the pesto, blend the garlic, salt, pine nuts, fresh basil leaves and grated Parmesan in a food processor or blender until thoroughly combined. With the motor running, add the oil in a thin steady stream and process until smooth.
2 Cook the orecchiette pasta in a large saucepan of rapidly boiling salted water for 12 minutes, or until *al dente*. Drain, transfer to a large bowl, then toss the pesto through.
3 Pat the drained capers dry with paper towels, then heat the olive oil in a frying pan and cook the capers for 4–5 minutes, stirring occasionally, until crisp. Remove and drain on paper towels.

4 Heat the extra virgin olive oil in a deep frying pan over medium heat and add the garlic, tomatoes and asparagus. Toss continuously for 1–2 minutes, or until warmed through. Stir in the balsamic vinegar.
5 When the pasta is just warm, not hot (otherwise it will wilt the rocket), toss the tomato mixture, rocket and prawns with the pasta and season with salt and freshly ground black pepper, to taste. Serve sprinkled with the cooled capers and the freshly shaved Parmesan.

NUTRITION PER SERVE
Protein 42 g; Fat 52 g; Carbohydrate 91.5 g; Dietary Fibre 10 g; Cholesterol 163 mg; 4195 kJ (1000 cal)

Use two wooden spoons to toss the pesto through the drained pasta.

Cook the capers in the hot oil, stirring occasionally, until crisp.

THAI NOODLE SALAD

Preparation time: 25 minutes
Total cooking time: 2 minutes
Serves 4

Dressing
2 tablespoons grated fresh ginger
2 tablespoons soy sauce
2 tablespoons sesame oil
80 ml (⅓ cup) red wine vinegar
1 tablespoon sweet chilli sauce
2 cloves garlic, crushed
80 ml (⅓ cup) kecap manis

500 g (1 lb 2 oz) cooked large prawns
(shrimp)
250 g (9 oz) dried instant egg noodles
5 spring onions (scallions), sliced
diagonally
2 tablespoons chopped coriander
(cilantro)
1 red capsicum (pepper), diced
100 g (3½ oz) snowpeas
(mangetout), sliced

1 For the dressing, whisk together
the fresh ginger, soy sauce, sesame oil,
red wine vinegar, chilli sauce, garlic
and kecap manis in a large bowl.

2 Peel the prawns and gently pull out
the dark vein from each prawn back,
starting at the head end. Cut each
prawn in half lengthways.
3 Cook the egg noodles in a large
saucepan of boiling water for
2 minutes, or until tender, then drain
thoroughly. Cool in a large bowl.
4 Add the dressing, prawns and
remaining ingredients to the noodles
and toss gently.

NUTRITION PER SERVE
Protein 31.5 g; Fat 11.5 g; Carbohydrate
48 g; Dietary Fibre 3.5 g; Cholesterol
175.5 mg; 1805 kJ (430 cal)

*Whisk all the dressing ingredients
together in a large bowl.*

*Cut each of the peeled, deveined prawns
in half lengthways.*

*Toss the noodles, prawns, dressing,
herbs and vegetables together.*

FRESH BEETROOT, SCALLOP AND GOATS CHEESE SALAD

Preparation time: 20 minutes
Total cooking time: 35 minutes
Serves 4

1 kg (2 lb 4 oz) fresh beetroot
    (about 4 bulbs with leaves)
200 g (7 oz) green beans, trimmed
1 tablespoon red wine vinegar
2 tablespoons extra virgin
    olive oil
1 clove garlic, crushed
1 tablespoon drained capers,
    coarsely chopped
400 g (14 oz) scallops, without roe
40 g (1½ oz) butter
100 g (3½ oz) goats cheese

1 Trim the leaves from the beetroot, scrub the bulbs and wash the leaves. Add the bulbs to a large saucepan of boiling water, reduce the heat and simmer, covered, for 30 minutes, or until tender when pierced with the point of a knife (cooking time will vary). Drain and cool, then peel the beetroot under cold running water. Cut the bulbs into thin wedges.
2 Bring a saucepan of water to the boil and cook the beans for 3 minutes, or until just tender. Remove with a slotted spoon and plunge into a bowl of cold water. Drain. Add the beetroot leaves to the boiling water and cook for 3–5 minutes, or until the leaves and stems are tender. Plunge into a bowl of cold water, then drain well.
3 Put the red wine vinegar in a screw top jar with the oil, garlic, capers, and ½ teaspoon each of salt and cracked black pepper. Shake well.
4 Pull or slice off any membrane,

vein or hard white muscle from the scallops. Melt the butter in a frying pan and cook the scallops for 1–2 minutes each side, or until cooked.
5 Divide the beans, beetroot leaves and bulbs among four plates. Crumble goats cheese over, then top with scallops. Drizzle with dressing.

NUTRITION PER SERVE
Protein 20 g; Fat 24.5 g; Carbohydrate 13.5 g; Dietary Fibre 5.5 g; Cholesterol 76 mg; 1455 kJ (345 cal)

Hold the beetroot under cold running water and pull off the skin.

Cook the beetroot leaves and stems until both are tender.

Turn the scallops over after 1–2 minutes and cook until cooked through.

SQUID AND SCALLOPS WITH HERB DRESSING

Preparation time: 30 minutes
  + 30 minutes chilling
Total cooking time: 10 minutes
Serves 4

2 oranges
8 baby squid
200 g (7 oz) scallops, without roe
2 tablespoons oil
150 g (5½ oz) rocket (arugula)
3 ripe Roma (plum) tomatoes, chopped

Herb Dressing
50 g (1 cup) finely chopped coriander
  (cilantro)
30 g (1 cup) finely chopped flat-leaf
  (Italian) parsley
2 teaspoons ground cumin
1 teaspoon paprika
60 ml (¼ cup) lime juice
60 ml (¼ cup) olive oil

1 Remove the skin and white pith from the oranges. Use a small sharp knife to cut between the membranes and divide into segments. Remove the seeds. Set aside.
2 To clean the squid, gently pull the tentacles away from the hoods (the intestines should come away at the same time). Remove the intestines from the tentacles by cutting under the eyes, then remove the beaks, if they remain in the centre of the tentacles, by using your finger to push up the centre. Pull away the soft bones (quill) from the hoods. Rub the hoods under cold running water and the skin should come away easily. Wash the hoods and tentacles and drain. Place in a bowl of water with ¼ teaspoon salt and mix well. Cover and refrigerate for about 30 minutes. Drain and cut the tubes into long thin strips and the tentacles into pieces.
3 Pull or slice off any membrane, vein or hard white muscle from the scallops. Rinse and pat dry.
4 Heat the oil in a large deep frying pan over high heat and cook the squid in batches for 1–2 minutes, or until it turns white. Do not overcook or it will be tough. Drain on paper towels. Add the scallops to the pan and cook for 1–2 minutes each side, or until tender. Do not overcook.
5 Arrange the rocket on a large platter, top with seafood, tomatoes and orange segments.
6 Whisk the dressing ingredients together in a non-metallic bowl, then pour over the seafood.

NUTRITION PER SERVE
Protein 29 g; Fat 26 g; Carbohydrate 8 g; Dietary Fibre 3.5 g; Cholesterol 265 mg; 1595 kJ (380 cal)

Release the orange segments by cutting through with a small sharp knife.

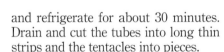

Gently pull the tentacles and intestines away from the squid hoods.

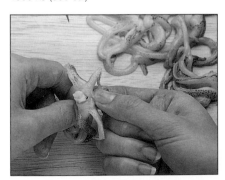

If the beak remains, remove it by using your finger to push up the centre.

SMOKED TROUT CAESAR SALAD

Preparation time: 15 minutes
Total cooking time: 20 minutes
Serves 4

80 ml (⅓ cup) extra virgin olive oil
2 cloves garlic, crushed
½ bread stick, thinly sliced
12 quail eggs
2 x 400 g (14 oz) whole smoked trout
2 cos (romaine) lettuce, torn into pieces
125 g (4½ oz) Parmesan, shaved

Dressing
250 g (1 cup) whole-egg mayonnaise
4 anchovy fillets, chopped, reserving 1 teaspoon oil
2 tablespoons lemon juice
2 cloves garlic, crushed, extra
2 tablespoons grated Parmesan

1 Preheat the oven to 180°C (350°F/Gas 4). Stir the oil and garlic together in a bowl. Brush over both sides of the bread slices and bake on a baking tray for 15 minutes, turning once, or until crisp and golden. Cool.
2 Cover the eggs with cold water in a saucepan. Bring to the boil and cook for 5 minutes. Put in a bowl of cold water to cool. Peel and cut each in half.
3 Place all the dressing ingredients in a food processor or blender and blend until smooth.
4 Remove the skin from the trout, pull the flesh from the bones and flake into pieces. Arrange the lettuce on plates and top with the trout. Spoon the dressing over, then top with the egg, shaved Parmesan and toast. Season with salt and ground black pepper, to taste.

NUTRITION PER SERVE
Protein 67 g; Fat 66 g; Carbohydrate 27 g; Dietary Fibre 2 g; Cholesterol 425.5 mg; 4065 kJ (970 cal)

Cut the bread into thin slices and bake on a baking tray until crisp and golden.

Process the dressing ingredients together until smooth.

Use a fork to flake the peeled trout flesh into pieces.

MAIN MEALS

BARBECUED TUNA AND MEDITERRANEAN VEGETABLES

Preparation time: 15 minutes
  + 30 minutes marinating
Total cooking time: 20 minutes
Serves 4

185 ml (¾ cup) olive oil
3 cloves garlic, crushed
2 tablespoons sweet chilli
    sauce
1 red capsicum (pepper), cut into
    3 cm (1¼ inch) pieces
1 yellow capsicum (pepper), cut into
    3 cm (1¼ inch) pieces
2 large zucchini (courgettes), cut into
    1.5 cm (⅝ inch) slices
2 slender eggplant (aubergines), cut
    into 1.5 cm (⅝ inch) slices
olive oil, extra, for brushing
4 tuna steaks

Lemon and Caper Mayonnaise
1 egg yolk
1 teaspoon grated lemon zest
2 tablespoons lemon juice
1 small clove garlic, chopped
185 ml (¾ cup) olive oil
1 tablespoon baby capers

1 Combine the olive oil, garlic and sweet chilli sauce in a large bowl. Add the capsicum, zucchini and eggplant, toss well, then marinate for 30 minutes.
2 For the mayonnaise, process the egg yolk, zest, lemon juice and garlic together in a food processor or blender until smooth. With the motor running, gradually add the oil in a thin steady stream until the mixture thickens and is a creamy consistency. Stir in the capers and ½ teaspoon salt. Set aside.
3 Heat the barbecue or a chargrill plate, brush with oil and cook the drained vegetables for 4–5 minutes each side, or until cooked through. Set aside and keep warm.
4 Brush the tuna steaks with extra oil and barbecue for 2–3 minutes each side, or until just cooked (tuna should be rare in the centre). Arrange the vegetables and tuna steaks on individual serving plates and serve with the mayonnaise.

NUTRITION PER SERVE
Protein 68 g; Fat 69 g; Carbohydrate 6 g;
Dietary Fibre 3 g; Cholesterol 151 mg;
3885 kJ (925 cal)

COOK'S FILE

ALTERNATIVE FISH: Atlantic salmon swordfish.

Process the mayonnaise mixture until smooth and creamy.

Turn the vegetables over when browned on one side, then cook through.

BAKED SNAPPER WITH LIME SAUCE

Preparation time: 30 minutes
Total cooking time: 45 minutes
Serves 4

1 whole large (2 kg/4 lb 8 oz)
    snapper, scaled and cleaned

Lime Sauce
60 g (2¼ oz) butter
2 tablespoons plain (all-purpose) flour
375 ml (1½ cups) chicken stock
1 teaspoon finely grated
    lime zest
80 ml (⅓ cup) lime juice
1 teaspoon sugar
60 ml (¼ cup) cream
1 tablespoon chopped chives

1 Preheat the oven to 180°C (350F/ Gas 4). Make 2 diagonal cuts in the thickest part of the fish on each side, then season the fish inside and out with salt and pepper. Wrap in foil, leaving a slight air pocket on top. Place on a baking tray and bake for 45 minutes, or until cooked (flesh will flake easily when tested with a fork).

2 Meanwhile, melt the butter in a saucepan over low heat. Stir in the flour and cook for 1 minute, or until pale and foaming. Remove from the heat and gradually stir in the combined chicken stock, zest, juice and sugar. Return to the heat and stir until the sauce boils and thickens. Stir in the cream and chives. Reduce the heat and simmer for 2 minutes. Season, to taste.

3 Carefully remove the fish from the foil, place on a serving platter and serve with the sauce. Slices of lime make an attractive garnish.

NUTRITION PER SERVE
Protein 32 g; Fat 21.5 g; Carbohydrate 6.5 g; Dietary Fibre 0.5 g; Cholesterol 151.5 mg; 1460 kJ (350 cal)

COOK'S FILE

ALTERNATIVE FISH: Ocean trout, red emperor, bream.

With a large knife, cut 2 diagonal slits in the thickest part of the fish on each side.

When the fish is cooked, the flesh will flake easily when tested with a fork.

Stir constantly with a wooden spoon until the sauce boils and thickens.

CAJUN BLACKENED FISH

Preparation time: 10 minutes
Total cooking time: 5 minutes
Serves 4

3 teaspoons paprika
1/2 teaspoon cayenne pepper
3 teaspoons black pepper
1 teaspoon white pepper
1 teaspoon dried thyme
50 g (1¾ oz) butter
4 x 200 g (7 oz) firm white fish fillets
2 cloves garlic, crushed
1 lemon, cut into wedges

1 Place the paprika, cayenne pepper, black pepper, white pepper and dried thyme in a bowl and mix well.
2 Melt the butter in a large frying pan over medium heat, then remove the pan from the heat. Brush both sides of the fillets with some of the melted butter, then spread the crushed garlic over the fish. Sprinkle each side of the fillets with the spice mixture.
3 Return the pan to medium heat and cook the fish for 1–2 minutes each side, or until cooked through (the fish will flake easily when tested with a fork). Spoon the pan juices over the fish and serve immediately with the lemon wedges on the side.

Brush the fish with butter, spread with garlic, then sprinkle the spices all over.

NUTRITION PER SERVE
Protein 38 g; Fat 15.5 g; Carbohydrate 3 g; Dietary Fibre 1.5 g; Cholesterol 158 mg; 1265 kJ (300 cal)

COOK'S FILE

SUGGESTED FISH: Deep-sea perch, ling, ocean perch.
NOTE: For less heat, you can omit the cayenne and white peppers.

Test the fish with a fork. When it is cooked, it will flake apart easily.

PRAWN AND COCONUT CURRY

Preparation time: 30 minutes
Total cooking time: 20 minutes
Serves 4

1 onion, chopped
2 cloves garlic, crushed
1 stem lemon grass, white part only, finely chopped
1/2 teaspoon sambal oelek
2 teaspoons garam masala
4 makrut (kaffir) lime leaves, finely shredded
3 tablespoons chopped coriander (cilantro) stems

1 tablespoon peanut oil
250 ml (1 cup) chicken stock
400 ml (14 fl oz) can coconut milk
1 kg (2 lb 4 oz) raw medium prawns (shrimp), peeled and deveined
1 tablespoon fish sauce
3 tablespoons coriander (cilantro) leaves, for serving

1 For the curry paste, place the onion, garlic, lemon grass, sambal oelek, garam masala, lime leaves, chopped coriander stems and 2 tablespoons water in a food processor and process until smooth.
2 Heat the oil in a saucepan, add the curry paste and cook for 2–3 minutes, or until fragrant. Stir in the stock and

coconut milk, bring to the boil, then reduce the heat and simmer for 10 minutes, or until slightly thickened.
3 Add the prawns and cook for 3–5 minutes, or until cooked through. Stir in the fish sauce. Sprinkle with fresh coriander leaves and serve over steamed rice.

NUTRITION PER SERVE
Protein 39 g; Fat 25.5 g; Carbohydrate 6 g; Dietary Fibre1.5 g; Cholesterol 261 mg; 1650 kJ (395 cal)

COOK'S FILE

NOTE: Instead of prawns, you can use bite-sized pieces of boneless ling or gemfish fillets. Cook for 3–5 minutes, or until cooked through.

Cut the lime leaves into fine shreds with a sharp knife.

Process the curry paste ingredients in a processor or blender until smooth.

Gently simmer the sauce over low heat until slightly thickened.

HERBED WHOLE SALMON

Preparation time: 15 minutes
Total cooking time: 35 minutes
Serves 6–8

1 teaspoon fennel seeds
2 tablespoons extra virgin
　　olive oil
2 cloves garlic, finely chopped
60 ml (¼ cup) white wine
¼ teaspoon sugar
1 teaspoon chopped dill
2 kg (4 lb 8 oz) whole salmon, scaled
　　and cleaned
1 lemon, sliced
10 g (¾ cup) dill sprigs

1 Preheat the oven to 190°C (375°F/ Gas 5). Place the fennel seeds in a dry frying pan and roast over high heat for 30–60 seconds or until fragrant; do not burn. Grind in a spice grinder to form a fine powder. Whisk in a bowl with the olive oil, garlic, wine, sugar and chopped dill.
2 Pat the fish dry with paper towels and make 2 diagonal cuts in the thickest part of the fish on each side. Season, then stuff lemon slices and dill sprigs into the cavity. Place enough foil to cover the fish on a lined baking tray. Place the fish on top and pour on the wine mixture. Wrap loosely and bake for 30–35 minutes, or until the dorsel fin pulls away easily

or the fish flakes easily when tested with a fork (salmon should be rare in the centre so it is moist).
3 Cut with a spoon on the natural marking along the fish, then across in sections and pull away from the bone (remove the skin if you like). Serve with lemon and dill butter (see page 84), or melted butter mixed with lemon juice and juices from the fish.

NUTRITION PER SERVE (8)
Protein 43 g; Fat 28.5 g; Carbohydrate 0.5 g; Dietary Fibre 0.5 g; Cholesterol 1210 mg; 1873 kJ (446 cal)

COOK'S FILE

SUGGESTED FISH: Ocean trout, snapper, bream.

Push the lemon slices and dill sprigs into the salmon cavity.

Put the fish on a serving plate and cut along the natural line with a spoon.

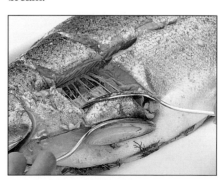

Cut sections across the fish with the spoon and pull away from the bone.

SALMON FILLETS WITH LEMON HOLLANDAISE SAUCE

Preparation time: 5 minutes
Total cooking time: 10 minutes
Serves 4

Lemon Hollandaise Sauce
175 g (6 oz) butter
4 egg yolks
2 tablespoons lemon juice

2 tablespoons olive oil
4 salmon fillets with skin on

1 Melt the butter in a small saucepan over low heat. Skim any froth from the surface and discard. Leave to cool. Whisk the yolks and 2 tablespoons water in a separate small saucepan for 30 seconds, or until pale and foamy. Place the saucepan over very low heat and whisk the egg mixture for 2–3 minutes, or until frothy and the whisk leaves a trail behind it as you whisk. Don't let the saucepan get too hot or you will scramble the eggs. Remove from the heat.
2 Whisk the cooled butter into the eggs, a little at a time, whisking well after each addition. Avoid using the milky butter whey from the base of the saucepan. Stir in the lemon juice and season with salt and cracked black pepper. Set aside.
3 Heat the oil in a large non-stick frying pan over high heat and cook the salmon fillets skin-side down for 2 minutes. Turn over and cook for 2 minutes, or until cooked to your liking. Serve with the sauce and vegetables of your choice.

NUTRITION PER SERVE
Protein 52.5 g; Fat 78 g; Carbohydrate 0.5 g; Dietary Fibre 0 g; Cholesterol 432 mg; 3860 kJ (920 cal)]

COOK'S FILE

ALTERNATIVE FISH: Tuna, blue-eye.
NOTE: Hollandaise sauce should be made in a heavy-based saucepan. If you make sure the egg yolks are whisked thoroughly, the next step of incorporating the clarified butter will be no trouble. You should end up with a thick emulsion. If the sauce separates or curdles, remove from the heat and whisk in an ice cube.

Use a spoon to carefully skim off any froth that forms on top of the butter.

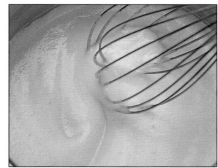

Whisk the egg yolks over very low heat until the whisk leaves a trail behind.

Add a little cooled butter at a time to the eggs, whisking well after each addition.

Use a spatula to turn the fillets over, then cook until done to your liking.

STEAMED FISH WITH GINGER

Preparation time: 10 minutes
Total cooking time: 15 minutes
Serves 4

4 whole bream, each about 350 g
    (12 oz), scaled and cleaned
2 tablespoons julienned ginger
60 ml (¼ cup) peanut oil
2–3 tablespoons soy sauce
6 spring onions (scallions), sliced
45 g (1½ oz) coriander (cilantro) sprigs

1 Make 2 diagonal cuts in the thickest part of each fish on both sides, then put in a lined bamboo or other large steamer. Cover and steam for 10 minutes, or until cooked (the fish will flake easily when tested with a fork).

2 Place each whole fish on a serving plate and scatter some of the fresh julienned ginger over the fish. Heat the oil in a small saucepan over medium heat until the oil begins to smoke. Pour some hot oil over each fish. The oil will sizzle and splatter, so stand back a little (the oil must be very hot or the fish won't go crisp and may seem oily). Drizzle the soy sauce over the fish and garnish with spring onion and coriander sprigs.

3 This fish is delicious served with steamed rice and steamed or stir-fried Asian vegetables.

NUTRITION PER SERVE
Protein 52.5 g; Fat 27.5 g; Carbohydrate 2 g; Dietary Fibre 1 g; Cholesterol 193 mg; 1950 kJ (465 cal)

COOK'S FILE

ALTERNATIVE FISH: Whole snapper, flounder.

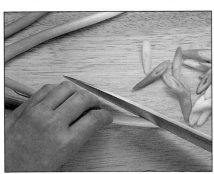

Cut the spring onions on the diagonal into short pieces.

When the fish is cooked it will flake apart easily when tested with a fork.

Put the cooked fish on serving plates and drizzle some hot oil over each.

FISH FILLETS IN CRISPY BATTER WITH SHIITAKE MUSHROOM SAUCE

Preparation time: 15 minutes
  + 15 minutes soaking
Total cooking time: 15 minutes
Serves 4

Shiitake Mushroom Sauce
50 g (1¾ oz) dried shiitake
  mushrooms
2 tablespoons peanut oil
2 cloves garlic, chopped
2 teaspoons chopped fresh ginger
1 small red chilli, deseeded and sliced
3 spring onions (scallions), sliced
  diagonally
2 tablespoons oyster sauce
2 tablespoons soy sauce
2 tablespoons Chinese wine
2 teaspoons sugar

Batter
60 g (½ cup) plain (all-purpose) flour
60 g (½ cup) cornflour (cornstarch)
1 teaspoon baking powder
1½ teaspoons salt

4 x 200 g (7 oz) flounder or sole fillets
plain (all-purpose) flour, for dusting
oil, for deep-frying
coriander (cilantro), to garnish

1 Soak the shiitake mushrooms in a bowl of boiling water for 10 minutes, or until soft. Drain, then cut off the stalks and thinly slice the mushrooms. Heat the oil in a frying pan or wok and cook the garlic, ginger and chilli over low heat for 1 minute, or until aromatic. Add the mushrooms and spring onion and cook for 1 minute over medium heat. Mix the oyster and soy sauces, Chinese wine, sugar and 60 ml (¼ cup) water in a bowl. Add to the frying pan and cook, stirring for 1–2 minutes, or until combined.
2 Sift all the dry ingredients for the batter into a bowl and make a well. Add 185 ml (¾ cup) chilled water and whisk until combined. Dry the fish with paper towels and dust with flour.
3 Fill a wok one third full of oil and heat to 180°C (350°F), or until a cube of bread browns in 15 seconds. Dip the fish in batter, drain off any excess and cook in batches for 5–6 minutes, or until the fish is golden and flakes when you test a small piece with a fork. Drain on crumpled paper towels.
4 Top the fish with sauce. Garnish and serve with greens and rice.

NUTRITION PER SERVE
Protein 43.5 g; Fat 20 g; Carbohydrate 41.5 g; Dietary Fibre 2.5 g; Cholesterol 131 mg; 2185 kJ (520 cal)

Cook the sauce until the ingredients are well combined.

COOK'S FILE

SUGGESTED FISH: Fillets of ling, flathead, sole.
NOTE: If the sauce is left to stand for too long, the mushrooms will soak up the liquid. If this happens, just add a little more water and reheat. If you prefer fresh shiitake mushrooms, slice 100 g (3½ oz) of them and add to the pan.

Remove the cooked fish from the oil with a slotted spoon.

MUSSELS IN CHUNKY TOMATO SAUCE

Preparation time: 15 minutes
Total cooking time: 30 minutes
Serves 4–6

1.5 kg (3 lb 5 oz) black mussels
3 tablespoons olive oil
1 large onion, diced
4 cloves garlic, finely chopped
810 g (1 lb 12 oz) can diced tomatoes
60 g (¼ cup) tomato paste (purée)
30 g (¼ cup) pitted black olives
1 tablespoon capers
125 ml (½ cup) fish stock
3 tablespoons chopped flat-leaf (Italian) parsley

1 Scrub the mussels with a stiff brush and pull out the hairy beards. Discard any damaged mussels, or those that don't close when tapped on the bench.

2 In a large saucepan, heat the olive oil and cook the onion and garlic over medium heat for 1–2 minutes, until softened. Add the tomato, tomato paste, olives, capers, and fish stock. Bring to the boil, then reduce the heat and simmer, stirring occasionally, for 20 minutes, or until the sauce is thick.

3 Stir in the mussels and cover the saucepan. Shake or toss the mussels occasionally, and cook for 4–5 minutes, or until the mussels begin to open. Once they have all opened, remove the pan from the heat. Discard any unopened mussels.

4 Just before serving, toss the chopped parsley through. Serve with crusty bread.

NUTRITION PER SERVE (6)
Protein 17 g; Fat 13.5 g; Carbohydrate 11 g; Dietary Fibre 3 g; Cholesterol 35 mg; 973 kJ (233 cal)

Simmer the chunky tomato sauce, stirring occasionally, until thick.

Cook the mussels until they open. Discard any that don't open.

CREAMY GARLIC SEAFOOD

Preparation time: 20 minutes
Total cooking time: 20 minutes
Serves 6

12 scallops, with roe
500 g (1 lb 2 oz) skinless firm white
    fish fillets
6 raw Balmain bugs or crabs
500 g (1 lb 2 oz) raw medium prawns
    (shrimp), peeled and deveined
50 g (1¾ oz) butter
1 onion, finely chopped
5–6 large cloves garlic, finely chopped
125 ml (½ cup) white wine
500 ml (2 cups) cream
1½ tablespoons Dijon mustard
2 teaspoons lemon juice
2 tablespoons flat-leaf (Italian) parsley

1 Slice or pull off any membrane or hard muscle from the scallops. Cut the fish into 2 cm (¾ inch) cubes. Cut the heads off the bugs, then use scissors to cut down around the sides of the tail so you can flap open the shell. Remove the flesh in one piece, then slice each piece in half. Refrigerate the seafood, covered, until ready to use.
2 Melt the butter in a frying pan and cook the onion and garlic over medium heat for 2 minutes, or until the onion is softened (be careful not to burn the garlic—it may turn bitter).
3 Add the wine to the pan and cook for 4 minutes, or until reduced by half. Stir in the cream, mustard, and lemon juice and simmer for 5–6 minutes, or until reduced to almost half.
4 Add the prawns to the pan and cook for 1 minute, then add the bug

meat and cook for another minute, or until white. Add the fish and cook for 2 minutes, or until cooked through (the flesh will flake easily when tested with a fork). Finally, add the scallops and cook for 1 minute. If any of the seafood is still not cooked, cook for another minute or so, but be careful not to overcook as this will result in tough flesh. Remove the frying pan from the heat and toss the parsley through. Season, to taste. Serve with salad and bread.

NUTRITION PER SERVE
Protein 38.5 g; Fat 45.5 g; Carbohydrate 4 g; Dietary Fibre 1 g; Cholesterol 316 mg; 2460 kJ (585 cal)

COOK'S FILE

SUGGESTED FISH: Perch, ling, bream, tuna, blue-eye.

Use strong kitchen scissors to cut through the sides of each bug tail.

Pull back the shell and pull out the flesh in one piece.

Simmer the sauce for about 5 minutes, or until reduced by almost half.

CALAMARI IN BLACK BEAN AND CHILLI SAUCE

Preparation time: 20 minutes
Total cooking time: 10 minutes
Serves 4

4 squid hoods
2 tablespoons oil
1 onion, cut into 8 wedges
1 red capsicum (pepper), sliced
115 g (4 oz) baby corn, cut in halves
3 spring onions (scallions), optional,
    cut into 3 cm (1¼ inch) lengths

Black Bean Sauce
3 teaspoons cornflour (cornstarch)
2 tablespoons canned salted black
    beans, washed, drained
2 small red chillies, deseeded
    and chopped
2 cloves garlic, finely chopped
2 teaspoons grated fresh ginger
2 tablespoons oyster sauce
2 teaspoons soy sauce
1 teaspoon sugar

1 Open out each squid hood. Score a shallow diamond pattern over the inside surface, without cutting through, then cut into 5 cm (2 inch) squares.
2 For the sauce, mix the cornflour with 125 ml (½ cup) water in a small bowl. Place the black beans in a bowl and mash with a fork. Add the chilli, garlic, ginger, oyster and soy sauces, sugar and the cornflour mix and stir.
3 Heat the oil in a wok or frying pan and stir the onion for 1 minute over high heat. Add the capsicum and corn and stir for another 2 minutes.
4 Add the squid to the wok and stir for 1–2 minutes, until the flesh curls up. Add the sauce and bring to the boil, stirring constantly until the

sauce thickens. Stir in the spring onion. Serve with steamed rice noodles.

NUTRITION PER SERVE
Protein 11.5 g; Fat 10.5 g; Carbohydrate 12.5 g; Dietary Fibre 3.5 g; Cholesterol 99.5 mg; 800 kJ (190 cal)

COOK'S FILE

VARIATION: Instead of squid, you can use fish, cuttlefish, prawns, octopus, or a combination.
NOTE: Black beans are available in cans in Asian food stores.

Score a shallow diamond pattern over the inside surface of each hood.

Toss the squid in the wok until the flesh curls up.

Add the sauce, bring to the boil and stir constantly until the sauce thickens.

EASY SEAFOOD PAELLA

Preparation time: 25 minutes
Total cooking time: 45 minutes
Serves 6

500 g (1 lb 2 oz) raw medium prawns
    (shrimp)
300 g (10½ oz) skinless firm white
    fish fillets
250 g (9 oz) black mussels
200 g (7 oz) calamari rings
60 ml (¼ cup) olive oil
1 large onion, diced
3 cloves garlic, finely chopped
1 small red capsicum (pepper),
    thinly sliced
1 small red chilli, deseeded
    and chopped, optional
2 teaspoons paprika
1 teaspoon ground turmeric
2 tomatoes, peeled and diced
1 tablespoon tomato paste (purée)
400 g (2 cups) long-grain rice
125 ml (½ cup) white wine
1.25 litres (5 cups) fish stock
3 tablespoons chopped flat-leaf
    (Italian) parsley, for serving
lemon wedges, for serving

1 Peel the prawns, leaving the tails intact. Gently pull out the dark vein from each prawn back, starting at the head end. Cut the fish fillets into 2.5 cm (1 inch) cubes. Scrub the mussels and pull out the hairy beards. Discard any broken mussels or those that don't close when tapped. Refrigerate the seafood, covered, until ready to use.
2 Heat the oil in a paella pan or a large deep frying pan (about 32 cm/ 13 inches diameter) with a lid. Add the onion, garlic, capsicum, and chilli to the pan and cook over medium heat for 2 minutes, or until the onion and capsicum are soft. Add the paprika, turmeric and 1 teaspoon salt and stir-fry for 1–2 minutes, or until aromatic.
3 Add the tomato and cook for 5 minutes, or until softened. Add the tomato paste. Stir in the rice until it is well coated.
4 Pour in the wine and simmer until almost absorbed. Add all the fish stock and bring to the boil. Reduce the heat and simmer for 20 minutes, or until almost all the liquid is absorbed into the rice. There is no need to stir the rice, but you may occasionally need to fluff it up with a fork to separate the grains.
5 Add the mussels to the pan, poking the shells into the rice, cover and cook for 2–3 minutes over low heat. Add the prawns and cook for 2–3 minutes. Add the fish, cover and cook for 3 minutes. Finally, add the calamari rings and cook for 1–2 minutes. By this time, the mussels should have opened— discard any unopened ones. The prawns should be pink and the fish should flake easily when tested with a fork. The calamari should be white, moist and tender. Cook for another 2–3 minutes if the seafood is not quite cooked, but avoid overcooking as the seafood will toughen and dry out.
6 Serve with parsley and lemon wedges. Delicious with a tossed salad.

NUTRITION PER SERVE
Protein 44.5 g; Fat 14.5 g; Carbohydrate 58.5 g; Dietary Fibre 3.5 g; Cholesterol 217 mg; 2360 kJ (560 cal)

COOK'S FILE

SUGGESTED FISH: Perch, ling.
NOTE: You can use just fish, or try other seafood such as scampi, octopus or crabs.

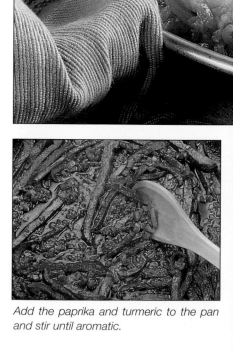

Protect your hands with rubber gloves when deseeding the chilli.

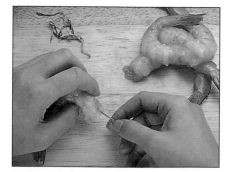

Pull out the dark vein from along the back of each prawn.

Add the paprika and turmeric to the pan and stir until aromatic.

Add the rice to the pan and stir with a wooden spoon until well coated.

Simmer the mixture until almost all the liquid is absorbed into the rice.

Cook the calamari rings for 1–2 minutes. Don't overcook or they will be tough.

SEAFOOD LASAGNE

Preparation time: 15 minutes
Total cooking time: 50 minutes
Serves 6

250 g (9 oz) fresh lasagne sheets
1 tablespoon olive oil
30 g (1 oz) butter
1 onion, finely chopped
2 cloves garlic, crushed
400 g (14 oz) raw medium prawns
  (shrimp), peeled and deveined
500 g (1 lb 2 oz) skinless firm white
  fish fillets, cut into 2 cm (3/4 inch)
  pieces
250 g (9 oz) scallops with roe,
  membrane removed
750 g (1 lb 10 oz) bottled tomato
  pasta sauce
1 tablespoon tomato paste (purée)
1 teaspoon soft brown sugar
60 g (1/2 cup) grated Cheddar
25 g (1/4 cup) grated Parmesan

Cheese Sauce
120 g (4 oz) butter
85 g (2/3 cup) plain (all-purpose) flour
1.5 litres (6 cups) milk
250 g (2 cups) grated Cheddar
100 g (1 cup) grated Parmesan

1 Preheat the oven to 180°C (350°F/ Gas 4). Lightly grease a 27 x 21 cm (11 x 8 1/2 inch), 2.5 litre (10 cup) ovenproof dish and line with lasagne sheets.
2 Heat the oil and butter in a large saucepan. Add the onion and cook for 2–3 minutes, or until softened. Add the garlic and cook for 30 seconds. Cook the prawns and fish pieces for 2 minutes, then add the scallops and cook for 1 minute. Stir in the pasta sauce, tomato paste and sugar and simmer for 5 minutes.

3 For the cheese sauce, melt the butter over low heat in a saucepan, stir in the flour and cook for 1 minute, or until pale and foaming. Remove from the heat and gradually stir in the milk. Return to the heat and stir until the sauce boils and thickens. Reduce the heat, simmer for 2 minutes, then stir in the cheeses. Season, to taste.
4 Spoon a third of the seafood sauce into the dish. Top with a third of the cheese sauce. Arrange lasagne sheets

over the top. Repeat to make three layers. Sprinkle with the cheeses and bake for 30 minutes or until golden. Leave for 10 minutes before slicing.

NUTRITION PER SERVE
Protein 70.5 g; Fat 63 g; Carbohydrate 50 g; Dietary Fibre 4.6 g; Cholesterol 332 mg; 4321 kJ (1033 cal)

C O O K ' S   F I L E

SUGGESTED FISH: Hake, snapper, flake, gemfish, ling.

Cut the fish fillets into even-sized pieces with a sharp knife.

Stir the sauce over low heat until it boils and thickens.

Layer lasagne sheets, seafood sauce and cheese sauce in the dish.

SPAGHETTI MARINARA

Preparation time: 40 minutes
Total cooking time: 50 minutes
Serves 6

Tomato Sauce
2 tablespoons olive oil
1 onion, finely chopped
1 carrot, sliced
2 cloves garlic, crushed
425 g (15 oz) can crushed tomatoes
125 ml (½ cup) white wine
1 teaspoon sugar

20 black mussels
60 ml (¼ cup) white wine
60 ml (¼ cup) fish stock
1 clove garlic, crushed
375 g (13 oz) spaghetti
30 g (1 oz) butter
125 g (4½ oz) calamari rings
125 g (4½ oz) skinless firm white
    fish fillets, cubed
200 g (7 oz) raw medium prawns,
    (shrimp) peeled and deveined
10 g (¼ oz) flat-leaf (Italian) parsley,
    chopped
200 g (7 oz) can clams, drained

1 For the sauce, heat the oil in a deep frying pan, add the onion and carrot and stir over medium heat for 10 minutes, or until the vegetables are golden. Add the garlic, tomato, wine and sugar and bring to the boil. Reduce the heat and gently simmer for 30 minutes, stirring occasionally.
2 Scrub the mussels and pull out the hairy beards. Discard any broken ones, or open ones that don't close when tapped. Rinse well. Heat the wine with the stock and garlic in a large frying pan. Add the mussels. Cover and shake the pan over high heat for 4–5 minutes. After 3 minutes, start removing opened mussels. After 5 minutes, discard any unopened mussels. Reserve the liquid.
3 Cook the spaghetti in a large pan of rapidly boiling salted water for 12 minutes, or until *al dente*. Drain.
4 Meanwhile, melt the butter in a frying pan, add the calamari, fish and prawns in batches and stir-fry for 2 minutes, or until just cooked through. Add the seafood to the tomato sauce with the reserved liquid, mussels, parsley and clams. Stir until the seafood is heated through. Add the

spaghetti to the pan and toss until well combined.

NUTRITION PER SERVE
Protein 34.5 g; Fat 14 g; Carbohydrate 51.5 g; Dietary Fibre 5 g; Cholesterol 139 mg; 2090 kJ (495 cal)

COOK'S FILE

SUGGESTED FISH: Blue-eye, groper, striped marlin.
NOTE: Buy the seafood and prepare your own marinara mix, rather than buying prepared marinara mixes.

Stir-fry the calamari rings, fish and prawns until just cooked through.

After adding the seafood and liquid to the sauce, stir until heated through.

FISH PIE

Preparation time: 10 minutes
Total cooking time: 1 hour
Serves 4

2 large potatoes, chopped
60 ml (¼ cup) milk or cream
1 egg
60 g (2¼ oz) butter
60 g (½ cup) grated Cheddar
800 g (1 lb 12 oz) white fish fillets, cut
    into large chunks
375 ml (1½ cups) milk, extra
1 onion, finely chopped
1 clove garlic, crushed
2 tablespoons plain (all-purpose) flour
2 tablespoons lemon juice
2 teaspoons lemon zest
1 tablespoon chopped dill

1 Preheat the oven to 180°C (350°F/ Gas 4). Boil or steam the potatoes for 8 minutes, or until tender. Drain and mash with the milk or cream, egg and half the butter. Mix in half the cheese, then set aside.

2 Put the fish in a shallow frying pan and cover with the extra milk. Bring to the boil, then reduce the heat and simmer for 2–3 minutes, or until the fish flakes easily. Drain the fish well, reserving the milk, and put in a 1.5 litre (6 cup) ovenproof dish.

3 Melt the remaining butter over medium heat in a saucepan and cook the onion and garlic for 2 minutes. Stir in the flour and cook for 1 minute, or until golden. Remove from the heat and gradually stir in the reserved milk. Return to the heat and stir constantly until the sauce boils and thickens. Reduce the heat and simmer for 2 minutes. Add the lemon juice, zest and dill, and season, to taste. Mix with the fish, cover with potato and sprinkle with the remaining cheese. Bake for 35 minutes, or until golden.

NUTRITION PER SERVE
Protein 54 g; Fat 29 g; Carbohydrate 24 g; Dietary Fibre 2.5 g; Cholesterol 253 mg; 2390 kJ (570 cal)

COOK'S FILE

SUGGESTED FISH: Ling, perch, hake, snapper.

Cook the fish in the simmering milk until it flakes easily when tested.

Stir the flour into the onion and garlic and cook until golden.

Using two spoons, cover the fish mixture with the mashed potato.

Whisk the flour and beer together until you have a smooth lump-free batter.

Cut the peeled potatoes into thick even-sized chips.

Cook the chips in batches a second time until crisp and golden.

If you need to turn the fish over during cooking, use tongs to handle.

FISH AND CHIPS

Preparation time: 25 minutes + soaking
Total cooking time: 30 minutes
Serves 4

155 g (1¼ cups) plain (all-purpose) flour
375 ml (1½ cups) beer
4 floury potatoes (e.g. spunta, russet or King Edward)
oil, for deep-frying
4 firm white fish fillets
cornflour (cornstarch), for coating
lemon wedges, for serving

1 Sift the flour into a large bowl, make a well and gradually add the beer, whisking to make a smooth lump-free batter. Cover and set aside. Preheat the oven to 180°C (350°F/Gas 4).
2 Cut the potatoes into 1 cm (¾ inch) thick chips. Soak in cold water for 10 minutes, drain and pat dry. Fill a deep heavy-based saucepan one third full of oil and heat to 160°C (315°F), or until a cube of bread browns in 30 seconds. Cook batches of chips for 4–5 minutes, or until pale golden. Remove with a slotted spoon. Drain on crumpled paper towels.
3 Just before serving, reheat the oil to 180°C (350°F), or until a cube of bread browns in 15 seconds. Cook the chips again, in batches, until crisp and golden. Drain. Keep hot on a baking tray in the oven.
4 Pat the fish dry with paper towels. Dust with cornflour, dip into the batter and drain off any excess. Deep-fry in batches for 5–7 minutes, or until cooked through. Turn with tongs if necessary. Remove with a slotted spoon and drain on crumpled paper towels. Serve with chips and lemon.

NUTRITION PER SERVE
Protein 22.5 g; Fat 18 g; Carbohydrate 51.5 g; Dietary Fibre 4 g; Cholesterol 49 mg; 2035 kJ (485 cal)

COOK'S FILE
SUGGESTED FISH: Fillets of bream, cod, coley, flake, flathead, pollack or snapper.

FLAVOURED BUTTERS

These butters melt into the hot seafood and are good to have on hand for adding zing to simply cooked fish or other seafood. All the butters can be stored, wrapped tightly, in the refrigerator for up to 1 week, or frozen for 2–3 months. The amounts are enough for 6 serves.

OLIVE, ANCHOVY AND CAPER

Beat 125 g (4½ oz) chopped, slightly softened unsalted butter with electric beaters until smooth. Beat in 2 teaspoons chopped capers, 3–4 chopped anchovy fillets and 1 tablespoon finely chopped green olives. Spoon onto greaseproof paper, shape into a 5 cm (2 inch) wide log, roll up and twist the ends to seal. Refrigerate until firm, then cut into 5 mm (⅛ inch) thick slices. Serve on fish such as poached salmon.

SEMI-DRIED TOMATO AND WHITE COSTELLO

Beat 90 g (3¼ oz) chopped, softened butter with electric beaters until smooth. Fold in 50 g (1¾ oz) finely chopped semi-dried (sun-blushed) tomatoes and 50 g (1¾ oz) chopped white costello cheese. Spoon onto greaseproof paper, shape into a 5 cm (2 inch) wide log, roll up and twist the ends to seal. Refrigerate until firm, then cut into 5 mm (⅛ inch) thick slices. Serve on seafood such as seared scallops.

LEMON AND DILL

Beat 100 g (3½ oz) unsalted chopped, softened butter with electric beaters until smooth. Beat in 2 teaspoons finely chopped dill, ½ teaspoon finely grated lemon zest and 2 tablespoons lemon juice until well combined. Spoon onto greaseproof paper, shape into a 5 cm (2 inch) wide log, roll up and twist the ends to seal. Refrigerate until firm, then cut into 5 mm (⅛ inch) thick slices. Serve on pan-fried fish such as bream.

ROASTED CAPSICUM AND ROCKET

Beat 125 g (4½ oz) chopped, softened butter with electric beaters until smooth. Fold through 1 large crushed garlic clove, 2 tablespoons finely chopped rocket (arugula) leaves, 1½ tablespoons finely chopped basil and 60 g (2¼ oz) roasted red capsicum (pepper), finely chopped, until combined. Spoon onto greaseproof paper, shape into a 5 cm (2 inch) wide log, roll up and twist the ends to seal. Refrigerate until firm, then cut into 5 mm (⅛ inch) thick slices. Serve on barbecued or chargrilled fish such as swordfish, tuna or blue-eye.

PESTO

Place 4 tablespoons basil leaves, 1 tablespoon each of pine nuts and grated Parmesan and 1 crushed garlic clove in a food processor or blender and process until smooth. Transfer to a bowl, add 125 g (4½ oz) chopped, softened butter and beat with a wooden spoon until combined. Spoon onto greaseproof paper, shape into a 5 cm (2 inch) wide log, roll up and twist the ends to seal. Refrigerate until firm. Cut into 5 mm (⅛ inch) thick slices and serve on top of barbecued or chargrilled tuna or swordfish steaks.

WASABI AND SEAWEED

Beat 125 g (4½ oz) chopped, softened butter with electric beaters until smooth. Fold through 2 teaspoons wasabi paste, 1 teaspoon rice vinegar and 1 sheet nori (dried seaweed), finely cut into small pieces with scissors. Spoon onto greaseproof paper, shape into a 5 cm (2 inch) wide log, roll up and twist the ends to seal. Refrigerate until firm, then cut into 5 mm (⅛ inch) thick slices. Serve on barbecued or chargrilled shellfish such as large prawns (shrimp).

SAFFRON AND PARSLEY

Grind ¼ teaspoon saffron threads in a mortar and pestle or spice grinder until powdery. Transfer to a small bowl, add 1 tablespoon hot water and soak for 2 minutes. Beat 125 g (4½ oz) chopped, softened butter with electric beaters until smooth. Beat in 2 teaspoons finely chopped parsley and the saffron and water. Spoon onto greaseproof paper, shape into a 5 cm (2 inch) wide log, roll up and twist the ends to seal. Refrigerate until required, then cut into 5 mm (⅛ inch) thick slices. Serve on fish such as pan-fried whiting or ocean perch fillets.

SWEET CHILLI AND CORIANDER

Beat 125 g (4½ oz) chopped, softened butter with electric beaters until smooth. Beat in 2 tablespoons sweet chilli sauce, 1 tablespoon chopped coriander (cilantro), ½ teaspoon grated fresh ginger and 1–2 teaspoons fish sauce. Spoon onto a piece of greaseproof paper, shape into a 5 cm (2 inch) wide log and roll up, twisting the ends to seal. Refrigerate until firm, then cut into 5 mm (⅛ inch) thick slices. Serve on shellfish such as barbecued or chargrilled prawns (shrimp).

Opposite page, from top: Olive, anchovy and caper;
Semi-dried tomato and white costello; Lemon and dill;
Roasted capsicum and rocket.
This page, from top: Pesto; Wasabi and seaweed;
Saffron and parsley; Sweet chilli and coriander.

SEAFOOD RISOTTO

Preparation time: 15 minutes
Total cooking time: 40 minutes
Serves 4

500 g (1 lb 2 oz) black mussels
200 g (2 oz) scallops
315 ml (1¼ cups) white wine
1.25 litres (5 cups) fish stock
pinch of saffron threads
2 tablespoons olive oil
30 g (1 oz) butter
500 g (1 lb 2 oz) raw prawns (shrimp),
    peeled and deveined
225 g (8 oz) calamari rings
3 cloves garlic, crushed
1 onion, finely chopped
440 g (2 cups) arborio rice
2 tomatoes, peeled and
    chopped
2 tablespoons chopped flat-leaf
    (Italian) parsley
125 ml (½ cup) cream

1 Scrub the mussels and pull away the hairy beards. Discard any broken mussels or those that don't close when tapped on the bench. Slice or pull off any vein, membrane or hard white muscle from the scallops.
2 Put the mussels in a saucepan, pour in the white wine, and cook, covered, over medium heat for 3–5 minutes, or until the mussels have opened (at this stage, discard any unopened ones). Strain, and reserve the liquid. Remove the mussels from the shells and discard the shells.
3 Combine the mussel liquid, fish stock and saffron in a saucepan, cover and keep at a low simmer.
4 Heat the oil and butter in a saucepan over medium heat, add the prawns and cook for 2–3 minutes, or until pink. Remove from the pan. Add the scallops and calamari rings to the saucepan and cook for 1–2 minutes, or until just cooked. Remove from the pan. Add the garlic and onion to the saucepan and cook for 3 minutes, or until golden and softened. Add the arborio rice and stir until well coated.
5 Add 125 ml (½ cup) hot liquid to the saucepan, stirring constantly, until the liquid is absorbed. Continue adding liquid, 125 ml (½ cup) at a time, stirring after each addition, until absorbed. It will take about 25 minutes

for all the stock to be absorbed. Stir in the seafood, tomato, parsley and cream until heated through. Season, to taste. Delicious with crusty bread.

NUTRITION PER SERVE
Protein 63.5 g; Fat 36 g; Carbohydrate 95 g; Dietary Fibre 4 g; Cholesterol 370 mg; 4235 kJ (1010 cal)

Cook the mussels over medium heat until they open. Discard any unopened ones.

Add the seafood, tomato, parsley and cream to the pan and stir through.

MALAYSIAN FISH CURRY

Preparation time: 25 minutes
Total cooking time: 25 minutes
Serves 4

2 cm x 4 cm (¾ x 1½ inch) piece
    fresh ginger
3–6 fresh medium red chillies
1 onion, chopped
4 cloves garlic, chopped
3 stems lemon grass, white part
    only, sliced
2 teaspoons shrimp paste
60 ml (¼ cup) oil
1 tablespoon fish curry powder
250 ml (1 cup) coconut milk
1 tablespoon tamarind concentrate

1 tablespoon kecap manis
500 g (1 lb 2 oz) firm white skinless
    fish fillets, cut into cubes
2 ripe tomatoes, chopped
1 tablespoon lemon juice

1 Slice the ginger and process in a small food processor with the chillies, onion, garlic, lemon grass and shrimp paste until roughly chopped. Add 2 tablespoons of the oil and process until a paste forms, regularly scraping the side of the bowl with a spatula.
2 Heat the remaining oil in a wok or deep, heavy-based frying pan and add the paste. Cook for 3–4 minutes over low heat, stirring constantly, until fragrant. Add the curry powder and stir for 2 minutes. Add the coconut milk, tamarind, kecap manis and 250 ml (1 cup) water. Bring to the boil, stirring occasionally, then reduce the heat and simmer for 10 minutes.
3 Add the fish, tomato and lemon juice. Season, to taste, then simmer for 5 minutes, or until the fish is just cooked (it will flake easily). Serve with steamed rice. Can be sprinkled with ready-made fried onion.

NUTRITION PER SERVE
Protein 30 g; Fat 31 g; Carbohydrate 11 g;
Dietary Fibre 4 g; Cholesterol 89 mg;
1810 kJ (430 cal)

COOK'S FILE

SUGGESTED FISH: Ling, flake, hake.
NOTE: Fish curry powder blend is available from speciality stores.

Add 2 tablespoons oil to the chilli mixture and process to a paste.

Add the curry powder to the wok and stir to incorporate.

Add the fish, tomato and lemon juice to the wok and simmer until the fish cooked.

GREEN FISH CURRY

Preparation time: 15 minutes
Total cooking time: 15 minutes
Serves 4

1 tablespoon peanut oil
1 brown onion, chopped
1½ tablespoons green
   curry paste
375 ml (1½ cups) coconut milk
700 g (1 lb 9 oz) boneless firm white
   fish fillets, cut in bite-sized pieces

3 makrut (kaffir) lime leaves
1 tablespoon fish sauce
2 teaspoons grated palm sugar
2 tablespoons lime juice
1 long green chilli, finely sliced

1 Heat a wok until very hot, add the oil and swirl to coat. Add the onion and stir-fry for 2 minutes, or until soft. Add the curry paste and stir-fry for 1–2 minutes, or until fragrant. Stir in the coconut milk and bring to the boil.
2 Add the fish and lime leaves to the wok, reduce the heat and simmer,

stirring occasionally, for 8–10 minutes, or until the fish is cooked through.
3 Stir in the fish sauce, palm sugar and lime juice. Scatter the chilli slices over the curry before serving with steamed rice.

NUTRITION PER SERVE
Protein 39 g; Fat 29 g; Carbohydrate 4.5 g; Dietary Fibre 1 g; Cholesterol 123.5 mg; 1820 kJ (435 cal)

COOK'S FILE

SUGGESTED FISH: Ling, ocean perch, bream, warehou.

To prevent skin irritation, wear rubber gloves when slicing the chilli.

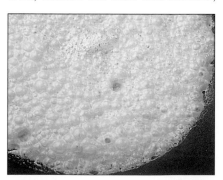

Heat the coconut milk to boiling point before adding the fish.

Gently simmer the fish pieces, stirring occasionally, until cooked through.

SEAFOOD CREPES

Preparation time: 30 minutes
 + 1 hour standing
Total cooking time: 45 minutes
Serves 6

85 g (²/₃ cup) plain (all-purpose) flour
250 ml (1 cup) milk
1 egg
15 g (½ oz) butter, melted
1 teaspoon sugar

Seafood Filling
300 g (10½ oz) raw medium prawns
 (shrimp), peeled and deveined
60 g (2¼ oz) unsalted butter
4 spring onions (scallions), finely
 chopped, white and green
 chopped separately
1 teaspoon Cajun spice mix
½ teaspoon sweet paprika
1 large tomato, chopped
125 ml (½ cup) dry white wine
170 g (6 oz) canned crab meat,
 drained, flaked
125 ml (½ cup) cream
1 tablespoon plain (all-purpose) flour
24 fresh oysters
2 tablespoons grated Cheddar

1 Sift the flour into a large bowl and make a well in the centre. Mix the milk, egg, butter and sugar in a bowl. Gradually add to the flour and whisk to make a smooth batter. Cover and stand for 1 hour.
2 For the filling, chop the prawns. Melt the butter in a frying pan, add the white part of the spring onion and cook, stirring over medium heat for 2 minutes. Add the spice mix, paprika and tomato, and cook, stirring, for 3–4 minutes. Add the wine and cook, stirring, until the sauce has thickened.

3 Stir the prawns and crab meat into the sauce and simmer for 2–3 minutes. Blend the cream and flour in a small bowl and add to the pan. Stir until the mixture boils and thickens. Add the oysters and spring onion greens. Remove from the heat.
4 Preheat the oven to 180°C (350°F/ Gas 4). Brush a 19 cm (7½ inch) crepe pan with butter or oil, then heat over moderate heat. Pour in 60 ml (¼ cup) batter and swirl to cover the base of the pan with batter. Cook until

bubbles form on top, then turn and cook until golden. Remove. Repeat to use all the batter, making 12 crepes. Stack them and cover with a cloth.
5 Spoon some seafood mixture onto each crepe and roll up. Arrange in a single layer in a greased ovenproof dish. Sprinkle with cheese and bake for 10 minutes, or until heated through.

NUTRITION PER SERVE
Protein 21.5 g; Fat 25 g; Carbohydrate 17 g; Dietary Fibre 1 g; Cholesterol 203.5 mg; 1625 kJ (385 cal)

Add the prawns and crab meat to the pan and simmer for 2–3 minutes.

When bubbles form on the surface, turn the crepe over and brown the other side.

Spoon some filling onto one end of each crepe and roll up to enclose.

LOBSTER CURRY WITH CAPSICUM

Preparation time: 25 minutes
Total cooking time: 15 minutes
Serves 4

2 raw lobster tails (350 g/12 oz each)
1 tablespoon oil
1–2 tablespoons red curry
    paste
2 stems lemon grass, white
    part only, finely chopped
1 red capsicum (pepper), roughly
    chopped
6 black dried Chinese dates
250 ml (1 cup) coconut milk
1 tablespoon fish sauce
2 teaspoons soft brown sugar
1 teaspoon grated lime zest
6 tablespoons coriander (cilantro)
    leaves, to garnish
lime wedges, to garnish,
    optional

1 Cut down the sides of the lobster tails on the underside. Remove the flesh and cut into 2 cm (3/4 inch) slices.
2 Heat the oil over medium heat in a wok or deep heavy-based frying pan. Add the curry paste and lemon grass and stir for 1 minute. Add the lobster pieces a few at a time and stir-fry each batch for 2 minutes, until golden brown and just cooked. Remove.
3 Add the capsicum to the wok and stir-fry for 30 seconds. Add the dates and coconut milk, bring to the boil and cook for 5 minutes, or until the dates are plump. Add the fish sauce, brown sugar and lime zest. Return the lobster pieces to the wok and heat through for 2–3 minutes. Garnish with coriander leaves and lime wedges and serve immediately with steamed rice.

NUTRITION PER SERVE
Protein 28 g; Fat 13 g; Carbohydrate 9 g;
Dietary Fibre 1.2 g; Cholesterol 136 mg;
1075 kJ (255 cal)

COOK'S FILE

HINTS: Asian food stores sell dried Chinese dates. Instead of lobster, you can use prawns or Balmain bug tails.

Use strong kitchen scissors to cut down the sides of the lobster tails.

Stir-fry batches of lobster pieces over medium heat until lightly golden.

Cook the dates for 5 minutes, or until they are plump.

THAI PRAWN CURRY

Preparation time: 30 minutes
Total cooking time: 10 minutes
Serves 4

2 cm x 2 cm (¾ x ¾ inch) piece fresh
    galangal
1 small onion, roughly chopped
3 cloves garlic
4 dried long red chillies
4 whole black peppercorns
2 tablespoons chopped lemon
    grass, white part only
1 tablespoon chopped coriander
    (cilantro) root

2 teaspoons grated lime zest
2 teaspoons cumin seeds
1 teaspoon sweet paprika
1 teaspoon ground coriander
3 tablespoons oil
1–2 tablespoons fish sauce
2 makrut (kaffir) lime leaves
500 ml (2 cups) coconut cream
1 kg (2 lb 4 oz) raw medium prawns
    (shrimp), peeled and deveined

1 Peel the galangal and thinly slice. Process the onion, garlic, chillies, peppercorns, lemon grass, coriander root, lime rind, cumin seeds, paprika, coriander, 2 tablespoons oil and ½ teaspoon salt in a small food processor until a smooth paste forms.

2 Heat the remaining oil in a frying pan. Add half the curry paste and stir over medium heat for 2 minutes. (Leftover curry paste can be kept in the refrigerator for up to 2 weeks.) Stir in the fish sauce, galangal, lime leaves and coconut cream.

3 Add the prawns to the pan and simmer for 5 minutes, or until the prawns are cooked and the sauce has thickened slightly. Serve with steamed jasmine rice.

NUTRITION PER SERVE
Protein 42 g; Fat 39.5 g; Carbohydrate 9 g; Dietary Fibre 4 g; Cholesterol 279.5 mg; 2310 kJ (550 cal)

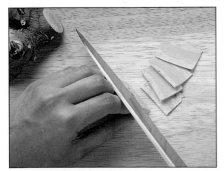

Peel the galangal and use a sharp knife to cut into very thin slices.

Add half the curry paste to the pan and stir over medium heat for 2 minutes.

Add the prawns to the pan and simmer until cooked.

SAUCES AND SALSAS

These sauces and salsas are a perfect accompaniment for a piece of cooked fish or other seafood.
Leftovers can be refrigerated in an airtight container for up to three days.

SALSA VERDE

Place 20 g (1 cup) tightly packed flat-leaf (Italian) parsley, 1 clove crushed garlic, 3 tablespoons dill, 2 tablespoons chopped chives and 4 tablespoons mint in a food processor and process for 30 seconds, or until combined. Add 1 tablespoon lemon juice, 5 anchovy fillets and 3 tablespoons drained, bottled capers and process until mixed. With the motor running, slowly add 125 ml (1/2 cup) olive oil in a thin stream and process until all the oil is added and the mixture is smooth. Serve with grilled prawns (shrimp) or fish kebabs (e.g. swordfish or salmon). Serves 4.

BUTTER SAUCE

Finely chop two French shallots and place in a small saucepan with 60 ml (1/4 cup) each of white wine vinegar and water. Bring to the boil, then reduce the heat and simmer until reduced to 2 tablespoons. Remove from the heat and strain into a clean saucepan. Return to the heat and whisk in 220 g (8 oz) cubed unsalted butter, a few pieces at a time. The sauce will thicken as the butter is added. Season, to taste, with salt, pepper and lemon juice. Serve with poached fish fillets such as salmon or barramundi, or barbecued lobster tail. Serves 4–6.

Clockwise, from bottom left: Salsa verde (in bowl and with prawns); Cannellini bean and semi-dried tomato salsa; Creamy tarragon sauce; Mango avocado salsa; Roasted capsicum and basil sauce; Butter sauce.

CANNELLINI BEAN AND SEMI-DRIED TOMATO SALSA

Drain a 400 g (14 oz) can cannellini beans and rinse the beans. Put in a bowl and stir with 75 g (½ cup) chopped semi-dried (sun-blushed) tomatoes, 30 g (¼ cup) sliced pitted black olives and ¼ red onion, chopped. Stir in 1 tablespoon olive oil, 3 teaspoons white wine vinegar and 1 tablespoon finely chopped flat-leaf (Italian) parsley. Cover and refrigerate for 30 minutes, or until required. Serve with fish such as baked red mullet or snapper. Serves 6.

ROASTED CAPSICUM AND BASIL SAUCE

Preheat the oven to 210°C (415°F/Gas 6–7). Halve two red capsicums (peppers) and place skin-side up on a greased baking tray with two cloves unpeeled garlic. Brush with olive oil and bake for 20 minutes, or until the capsicum is soft and the skin is blackened and blistered. Remove and cool the capsicums in a plastic bag. Peel the capsicums and garlic and mix in a food processor or blender for 30 seconds, or until combined. With the motor running, slowly add 100 ml (3½ fl oz) olive oil in a thin stream and blend until all the oil is added and the mixture is smooth. Add 1 tablespoon finely chopped basil, ¼ teaspoon salt and freshly ground black pepper. Serve warm or cold with barbecued fish such as sardines, swordfish or tuna. Serves 4.

CREAMY TARRAGON SAUCE

Combine 125 ml (½ cup) fish stock in a small saucepan with 1 crushed clove garlic, 1 teaspoon dried tarragon leaves and 1 thinly sliced spring onion (scallion). Bring to the boil, then reduce the heat and simmer for 3 minutes, or until reduced by half. Add 250 ml (1 cup) thick (double/heavy) cream or mascarpone. Reduce the heat to very low and stir until the cream has fully melted. Add ½ teaspoon lemon juice, 2 tablespoons grated Parmesan and salt and ground black pepper, to taste. Simmer for 1 minute, then serve with grilled (broiled) fish cutlets such as blue-eye. Serves 4–6.

MANGO AVOCADO SALSA

Cut 1 mango and 1 avocado into 1 cm (¾ inch) cubes and place in a small bowl with 1 diced small red capsicum (pepper). Mix 2 tablespoons lime juice with 1 teaspoon caster (superfine) sugar and pour over the mango. Stir in 3 tablespoons chopped coriander (cilantro) leaves. Serve with chilled cooked seafood such as prawns (shrimp). Serves 6.

SEAFOOD TERRINE

Preparation time: 30 minutes
+ overnight refrigeration
Total cooking time: 50 minutes
Serves 4–6

600 g (1 lb 5 oz) medium raw prawns
(shrimp)
400 g (14 oz) smoked salmon
400 g (14 oz) ocean trout fillet, skin
and bones removed
2 egg whites
125 ml (½ cup) cream
2 tablespoons chopped dill
50 g (1¾ oz) butter
3 cloves garlic, crushed
150 g (5½ oz) rocket (arugula)
400 g (14 oz) firm white fish fillets
rocket (arugula), extra, for serving

Aïoli
1 egg yolk
1 large clove garlic
2 teaspoons lemon juice
125 ml (½ cup) olive oil

1 Peel the prawns and gently pull out the dark vein from each prawn back. Grease a 1-litre (4 cup) rectangular ovenproof dish and line the base and sides with the smoked salmon, leaving some overhanging the sides. Preheat the oven to 180°C (350°F/Gas 4).
2 Roughly chop the ocean trout in a food processor or blender. Add the egg whites, cream, dill, salt and freshly ground black pepper and process until smooth.
3 Roughly chop the prawns. Melt the butter in a frying pan over high heat, add the garlic and prawns and cook for 4–5 minutes, or until just cooked.
4 Spread half the trout mixture over the smoked salmon. Cover with half

the rocket, then half the prawns and all of the fish. Repeat with the remaining ingredients and fold the salmon over to cover. Cover with a piece of greased baking paper, then put foil across the top and firmly seal.
5 Stand the terrine in a baking dish and pour in water to come about halfway up the sides of the terrine. Bake for 45 minutes, or until it feels firm when pressed.
6 Meanwhile, to make the aïoli, process the egg yolk with the garlic and the lemon juice in a small food processor or blender for 10 seconds, or until combined. With the motor running, slowly add the olive oil in a thin steady stream until the mixture is thick and creamy. Season with salt and freshly ground black pepper, to taste. Cover and refrigerate until ready to use.
7 Remove the terrine from the oven and cool slightly. Carefully drain away any excess liquid. Place a piece of cardboard on top of the terrine and weigh it down with weights or small food cans. Refrigerate overnight.
8 When ready to serve, carefully turn the terrine out of the dish and cut into slices. Drizzle with the aïoli and serve with extra rocket.

NUTRITION PER SERVE (6)
Protein 64 g; Fat 46 g; Carbohydrate 1.2 g;
Dietary Fibre 1 g; Cholesterol 330.5 mg;
2796 kJ (667 cal)

COOK'S FILE

SUGGESTED FISH: Salmon, perch, ling.
NOTE: The aïoli can be made up to 2 days in advance and stored in the refrigerator. To make it without a processor, whisk the egg yolk, garlic and lemon juice together, then whisk in the oil in a thin stream until thick.

The terrine is also delicious served with a home-made or bought pesto.

Line the dish with smoked salmon, leaving some overhanging the sides.

Process the trout with the egg whites, cream, dill, salt and pepper until smooth.

Cover the trout mixture with half the rocket, then half the cooked prawns.

When all the ingredients have been used, fold the salmon over the top to cover.

For the aïoli, add the oil in a thin stream until the mixture is creamy and thick.

Put cardboard on top of the terrine, weigh it down with cans and refrigerate.

SALMON WITH PASTA AND SAFFRON CREAM SAUCE

Preparation time: 15 minutes
Total cooking time: 20 minutes
Serves 4

500 g (1 lb 2 oz) pappardelle pasta
50 g (1¾ oz) butter
4 cloves garlic, crushed
150 g (5½ oz) oyster mushrooms
800 g (1 lb 12 oz) raw medium
  prawns (shrimp), peeled
  and deveined
2 x 400 g (14 oz) salmon fillets,
  skin removed, cut into
  2.5 cm (1 inch) cubes
250 ml (1 cup) white wine
250 ml (1 cup) fish stock
¼ teaspoon saffron threads
400 ml (14 fl oz) crème fraîche
125 g (4½ oz) sugar snap peas

1 Cook the pasta in a large saucepan of rapidly boiling salted water for 12 minutes, or until *al dente*. Drain and keep warm.
2 Meanwhile, melt the butter in a large deep frying pan, add the garlic and oyster mushrooms and cook for 1 minute. Add the prawns and salmon and cook for 2–3 minutes, or until the prawns are cooked and the salmon starts to flake but is still rare in the centre. Be careful not to burn the garlic. Transfer to a bowl.
3 Pour the wine and stock into the pan and add the saffron. Scrape the base of the pan to remove sediment. Bring to the boil, then reduce the heat and simmer rapidly for 5 minutes, or until reduced by half. Add the crème fraîche and sugar snap peas and stir through. Bring to the boil, then reduce the heat and simmer, stirring occasionally, for 3–4 minutes, until the liquid has slightly thickened.
4 Return the seafood mixture and any juices to the pan and gently stir over medium heat until warmed through. Divide the pasta among four plates and spoon the seafood and sauce over it. Season, to taste, and serve immediately.

NUTRITION PER SERVE
Protein 98 g; Fat 48 g; Carbohydrate 95.5 g; Dietary Fibre 9.5 g; Cholesterol 456 mg; 5240 kJ (1250 cal)

Cook the mushrooms, garlic, prawns and salmon until the fish just starts to flake.

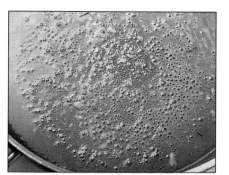

Add the wine, stock and saffron to the pan. Scrape the sediment from the base.

Simmer the mixture, stirring occasionally, until the sauce has slightly thickened.

Stir the sliced onion with a wooden spoon until slightly caramelized.

Reduce the heat and simmer until the liquid coats the back of a spoon.

Put some fish in each dish, dividing the pieces equally among the four dishes.

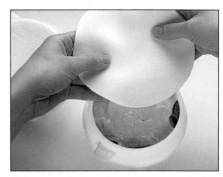

Put a round of pastry on top of each dish and gently press the edges.

CREAMY SNAPPER PIES

Preparation time: 25 minutes
Total cooking time: 1 hour 20 minutes
Serves 6

2 tablespoons olive oil
4 onions, thinly sliced
375 ml (1½ cups) fish stock
875 ml (3½ cups) cream
1 kg (2 lb 4 oz) skinless snapper
    fillets, cut into bite-sized pieces
2 sheets ready-rolled puff pastry,
    thawed
1 egg, lightly beaten

1 Preheat the oven to 220°C (425°F/ Gas 7). Heat the oil in a large deep-sided frying pan, add the onion and stir over medium heat for 20 minutes, or until the onion is golden brown and slightly caramelized.

2 Add the stock to the pan, bring to the boil and cook for 10 minutes, or until the liquid has nearly evaporated. Stir in the cream, bring to the boil, then reduce the heat and simmer for 20 minutes, or until the liquid reduces by half or coats the back of a spoon.
3 Divide half the sauce among six 315 ml (1¼ cup) deep ovenproof dishes. Put some fish in each dish, then top with the sauce.
4 Cut the pastry sheets into rounds slightly larger than the tops of the dishes. Brush the edges of the pastry with a little of the egg. Press onto the dishes. Brush lightly with the remaining beaten egg. Bake for 30 minutes, or until the pastry is crisp, golden and puffed.

NUTRITION PER SERVE
Protein 43 g; Fat 85 g; Carbohydrate 27 g; Dietary Fibre 1.6 g; Cholesterol 345 mg; 4347 kJ (1033 cal)

COOK'S FILE

ALTERNATIVE FISH: Fillets of bream, sea perch, ling or jewfish. Make sure you remove any bones before cooking.

BATTERS AND COATINGS

When delicious seafood is dipped in flavourful batters or coatings before being cooked, it not only has an extra dimension but retains its moisture and is therefore wonderfully succulent. All these recipes serve four.

SPICY BATTER

Sift 125 g (1 cup) plain (all-purpose) flour into a bowl with 2 teaspoons ground cumin, 2 teaspoons ground coriander, 1 teaspoon chilli powder and ¼ teaspoon ground turmeric. Make a well in the centre and slowly mix in 185 ml (¾ cup) water and 1 beaten egg. Mix well and set aside for 10 minutes. Fill a deep-fryer or deep, heavy-based saucepan one third full of oil and heat to 180°C (350°F), or until a cube of bread dropped into the oil browns in 15 seconds. Dip 500 g (1 lb 2 oz) John dory or flounder fillets in the batter and deep-fry for 2–3 minutes, or until golden and cooked through (the fish will flake easily—test a small piece with a fork). Drain on crumpled paper towels and serve immediately.

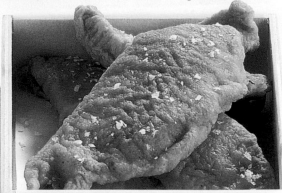

SEAWEED BATTER

Shred 1 sheet nori (dried seaweed) into fine strips with scissors. Place in a bowl and mix with 125 g (1 cup) tempura flour and 1 tablespoon sesame seeds. Make a well in the centre and gradually pour in 250 ml (1 cup) iced water. Mix gently until just combined (the batter will be lumpy). Fill a deep-fryer or deep, heavy-based saucepan one third full of oil and heat to 180°C (350°F), or until a cube of bread dropped into the oil browns in 15 seconds. Dip 500 g (1 lb 2 oz) small, firm, boneless white fish fillets (e.g. ling, perch), or raw medium, peeled prawns (shrimp) with tails intact, or calamari rings, in the batter, shaking off any excess. Deep-fry for 1–2 minutes, or until cooked through (the fish will flake easily—test a small piece with a fork). Drain on crumpled paper towels and serve with a bowl of shoyu (Japanese soy) mixed with a little wasabi paste.

SODA WATER BATTER

Sift 125 g (1 cup) plain (all-purpose) flour into a large bowl with ¼ teaspoon salt and finely ground black pepper. Make a well in the centre, pour in 250 ml (1 cup) chilled soda water and mix until just combined (the batter will be lumpy). Beat 1 egg white in a bowl to soft peaks and fold through the batter. Fill a deep-fryer or deep, heavy-based saucepan one third full of oil and heat to 180°C (350°F), or until a cube of bread dropped into the oil browns in 15 seconds. Dip 500 g (1 lb 2 oz) firm white fish fillets (e.g. ocean perch or whiting) in the batter, then deep-fry for 3–4 minutes, until crisp and lightly golden and cooked through (the fish will flake easily—test a small piece with a fork). Drain on crumpled paper towels, season with salt and serve immediately. This batter can also be used with prawns (shrimp) and vegetables.

BLACK SESAME CRUST

Mix 2 tablespoons black sesame seeds with 90 g (1½ cups) Japanese breadcrumbs in a bowl. Lightly beat an egg in a shallow bowl. Dust 500 g (1 lb 2 oz) firm white boneless fish fillets (e.g. ling, bream, ocean perch) in seasoned flour, dip lightly in the egg, then press in the breadcrumbs to coat well. Refrigerate for 30 minutes. Heat enough oil in a large deep frying pan to coat the base. Cook the fish for 2–3 minutes, or until golden brown and cooked through (the fish will flake easily when tested with a fork). Drain on crumpled paper towels and serve immediately. A dipping sauce can be made by mixing 125 g (½ cup) Japanese or whole-egg mayonnaise with 2 teaspoons wasabi paste and 3 teaspoons soy sauce in a bowl.

PARMESAN CRUST

Process 4 slices of fresh white bread, crusts removed, in a food processor for 30 seconds to make breadcrumbs. Combine in a large bowl with 140 g (1 cup) roughly chopped, roasted macadamias and 50 g (½ cup) grated Parmesan. Season with plenty of salt and pepper. Lightly beat an egg in a shallow bowl. Dust 500 g (1 lb 2 oz) salmon fillets or ocean perch with seasoned flour, dip into the egg, then press in the breadcrumb mixture to coat well. Refrigerate for 30 minutes. Heat enough oil in a large deep frying pan to coat the base. Cook the salmon, over medium heat, for 3–4 minutes on each side, until cooked through (the fish will flake easily—test a small piece with a fork). The coating should be crunchy and golden. Serve immediately.

CHILLI CRUST

Process 6 slices of fresh white bread, crusts removed, in a food processor for 30 seconds to make breadcrumbs. Combine in a large bowl with 3 teaspoons each of chilli flakes and ground cumin and a pinch of chilli powder. Season with salt and pepper. Lightly beat an egg in a shallow bowl. Pat dry 500 g (1 lb 2 oz) calamari rings, or 750 g (1 lb 10 oz) raw medium prawns (shrimp), peeled and deveined, with paper towels. Dust with flour, then dip in the egg and roll in the breadcrumbs, pressing to coat. Refrigerate for 30 minutes. Fill a deep-fryer or deep, heavy-based saucepan one third full of oil and heat to 180°C (350°F), or until a cube of bread dropped into the oil browns in 15 seconds. Deep-fry the calamari or prawns for 1 minute, or until golden and cooked. Drain on crumpled paper towels and serve.

Opposite page, from top: Spicy batter (with fish); Seaweed batter (with fish); Soda water batter (with prawns/shrimp and vegetables). This page, from top: Black sesame crust (with fish); Parmesan crust (with fish); Chilli crust (with calamari).

CHILLI CRAB

Preparation time: 20 minutes
Total cooking time: 15 minutes
Serves 4

1 kg (2 lb 4 oz) raw blue swimmer
    crabs
2 tablespoons peanut oil
2 cloves garlic, finely chopped
2 teaspoons finely chopped
    fresh ginger
2 small red chillies, seeded and sliced
2 tablespoons hoisin sauce
125 ml (½ cup) tomato sauce
60 ml (¼ cup) sweet chilli sauce
1 tablespoon fish sauce
½ teaspoon sesame oil
4 spring onions (scallions), finely
    sliced, to garnish, optional

1 Pull back the apron and remove the top shell from each crab. Remove the intestines and grey feathery gills. Segment each crab into 4 pieces. Crack the claws open with a crab cracker to allow the flavours to enter the crab meat and also to make it easier to eat the crab.

2 Heat a wok until very hot, add the oil and swirl to coat. Add the garlic, ginger and chilli and stir-fry for 1–2 minutes.

3 Add the crab pieces and stir-fry for 5–7 minutes, or until the meat turns white. Stir in the hoisin, tomato, sweet chilli and fish sauces, the sesame oil and 60 ml (¼ cup) water. Bring to the boil, then reduce the heat and simmer, covered, for 6 minutes, or until the crab flesh is cooked through and flakes easily.

4 Arrange on a platter and garnish with spring onion. Serve with steamed rice. Bowls of water with slices of lemon make it easy for people to rinse their messy fingers.

NUTRITION PER SERVE
Protein 17 g; Fat 12 g; Carbohydrate 19 g;
Dietary Fibre 3 g; Cholesterol 105 mg;
1045 kJ (250 cal)

C O O K ' S   F I L E

VARIATION: You can use any variety of raw crab meat for this recipe, or use prawns or Balmain bugs instead.
NOTE: If you prefer a hotter taste in your sauce, leave the seeds and membrane in the chillies.

Pull the apron back from the crabs and remove the top shell from each.

Pull out and discard the intestines and grey feathery gills.

Use a sharp, strong knife to cut each crab into four pieces.

After adding the sauces, oil and water, cook until the crab flesh flakes easily.

LOBSTER MORNAY

Preparation time: 25 minutes
+ 15 minutes standing
Total cooking time: 10 minutes
Serves 2

1 cooked medium lobster
315 ml (1¼ cups) milk
1 slice onion
1 bay leaf
6 black peppercorns
30 g (1 oz) butter
2 tablespoons plain (all-purpose) flour
2 tablespoons cream
60 g (2¼ oz) Cheddar, grated

1 Using a large sharp knife, cut the lobster in half lengthways through the tail. Lift the lobster meat from the tail and body, reserving both pieces of shell. Crack the legs and prise the meat out. Discard the cream vein and soft body matter. Cut the meat into 2 cm (¼ inch) pieces, cover and refrigerate. Wash and dry the shells.
2 Put the milk, onion, bay leaf and peppercorns in a saucepan. Bring to the boil, then remove from the heat, cover and leave for 15 minutes. Strain.
3 Melt the butter in a saucepan over low heat, stir in the flour and cook for 1 minute, or until pale and foaming. Remove from the heat and gradually stir in the strained milk. Return to the heat and stir until the mixture thickens. Reduce the heat to very low and simmer for 1 minute. Stir in the cream. Season, to taste, with salt and pepper, then fold in the lobster meat and stir over low heat for 1 minute, or until warmed through.
4 Spoon half the mixture into each shell and sprinkle with cheese. Cook the lobster under a hot griller (broiler) for 2 minutes, or until the cheese is golden. Can be served with asparagus.

NUTRITION PER SERVE
Protein 33.5 g; Fat 38 g; Carbohydrate 17.5 g; Dietary Fibre 1 g; Cholesterol 215.5 mg; 2270 kJ (540 cal)

Use a strong knife to cut the lobster in half lengthways through the tail.

Crack the lobster legs and prise the meat out with a knife.

Add the lobster meat to the sauce and stir over low heat until heated through.

101

SALMON STRIPS WITH DILL BATTER

Preparation time: 15 minutes
+ 20 minutes standing
Total cooking time: 40 minutes
Serves 4

90 g (¾ cup) plain (all-purpose) flour
½ teaspoon baking soda
½ teaspoon salt
1 tablespoon vinegar
2 tablespoons chopped dill
800 g (1 lb 12 oz) skinless salmon fillets
80 ml (⅓ cup) oil

1 To make the dill batter, sift the flour, baking soda and salt into a bowl and make a well in the centre. Add the vinegar combined with 185 ml (¾ cup) water and whisk into the flour until smooth. Cover with plastic wrap and set aside for 20 minutes. Stir in the chopped dill.

2 Meanwhile, remove any remaining bones from the salmon fillets with tweezers and cut each fillet into 4 strips. Preheat the oven to 160°C (315°F/Gas 2–3).

3 Heat the oil in a large frying pan. Dip the salmon strips in the dill batter and shake off any excess. Cook in 4 batches in the hot oil for 5 minutes each side (depending on the thickness of the fish), or until golden and cooked through. Drain the first batch on crumpled paper towel and keep warm in the oven while cooking the rest of the fish. Delicious with steamed vegetables and potato wedges.

NUTRITION PER SERVE
Protein 46.5 g; Fat 32.5 g; Carbohydrate 16.5 g; Dietary Fibre 1 g; Cholesterol 156 mg; 2270 kJ (540 cal)

COOK'S FILE

ALTERNATIVE FISH: Ling, swordfish or tuna fillets.

When the batter has been standing for 20 minutes, stir in the chopped dill.

Remove any bones from the fish, then cut each fillet into four strips.

Turn the strips over after 5 minutes, depending on the thickness of the fish.

DEEP-FRIED WHOLE FISH WITH ASIAN FLAVOURINGS

Preparation time: 20 minutes
Total cooking time: 25 minutes
Serves 4

Sauce
2 tablespoons chilli jam
2 makrut (kaffir) lime leaves, finely
    shredded
2 tablespoons fish sauce
1 teaspoon sesame oil
2 stems lemon grass, white
    part only, finely chopped
1 tablespoon finely grated fresh ginger
1 clove garlic, crushed
2 tablespoons shaved palm sugar
2 tablespoons lime juice
80 ml (⅓ cup) rice wine vinegar
1 tablespoon chopped coriander
    (cilantro) roots

4 x 350 g (12 oz) whole snapper or
    bream, cleaned and scaled
cornflour (cornstarch), for dusting
oil, for deep-frying
coriander (cilantro) sprigs, to garnish,
    optional
spring onions (scallions), to garnish,
    optional

1 Stir the sauce ingredients together with 2 tablespoons water in a small saucepan over medium heat. Bring to the boil and cook for 2 minutes, or until the sauce is reduced and slightly caramelized. Keep warm.
2 Score a shallow diamond pattern on both sides of each fish. Pat dry with paper towels and lightly coat in the cornflour, shaking off any excess.
3 Fill a wok or a deep heavy-based saucepan one third full of oil and heat to 180°C (350°F), or until a cube of bread dropped into the oil browns in 15 seconds. Cook each fish for 5 minutes, or until golden brown and cooked through. You may need to turn the fish with tongs or a long-handled spoon. Drain on crumpled paper towels and season. Serve immediately with the sauce. Whole fish look attractive served on banana leaves.

Garnish with coriander and raw or grilled (broiled) spring onions.

NUTRITION PER SERVE
Protein 57.5 g; Fat 26 g; Carbohydrate 17.5 g; Dietary Fibre 1.5 g; Cholesterol 214.5 mg; 2240 kJ (535 cal)

COOK'S FILE

NOTE: Chilli jam is available from Asian speciality stores.

Cook the sauce ingredients until reduced and slightly caramelized.

Cut a shallow diamond pattern into both sides of each fish with a sharp knife.

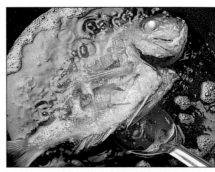

Cook the fish until cooked through, then remove with a slotted spoon.

SPECIES	ALSO KNOWN AS	CHARACTERISTICS
anchovies	smig	soft, oily flesh; strong flavour
Atlantic salmon	salmon trout	firm, oily, moist, orangy-pink flesh; distinctive flavour
Australian halibut	Queensland halibut	dry, white flesh; good flavour
barramundi		moist, white flesh, large flakes, fine bones; mild flavour
blue-eye	blue-eye cod, blue-eye trevalla, deep-sea trevalla, sea trevally, deep-sea trevally	moist, firm, white flesh, large bones; mild flavour
blue grenadier		fine, soft, white flesh; mild flavour
bonito	horse mackerel	firm flesh; mild flavour
bream	porgy, silver or black bream	soft, moist, white flesh; mild, sweet flavour
cod, Murray		firm, moist, white flesh, medium flakes; mild flavour
dhufish	perl perch	soft, white flesh; delicate, sweet flavour
emperor		firm, white flesh; mild flavour
flathead		dry, white flesh, medium flakes, bony; distinctive flavour
flounder		soft, moist, white flesh; delicate flavour
garfish	sea garfish, needlefish	soft, fine, white flesh, small soft bones; delicate, sweet flavour
garfish, snub-nosed	short-beaked, snub gar	fine texture, small soft bones; delicate, sweet flavour
gemfish	hake, southern kingfish	firm, moist, creamy-pink flesh, large flakes; mild flavour
groper	hapuka, bass groper	firm flesh; good flavour
gurnard		dry, fine, white flesh; mild flavour
herring		soft, oily, dark flesh; strong flavour
jewfish	mulloway, butterfish, silver jew, jewie	firm, white flesh, large flakes, can be dry; mild flavour
John dory	St Peter's fish, Kuparu	fine, firm, moist flesh; sweet flavour
kingfish	yellowtail kingfish, southern yellowtail, southern yellowfish	delicate, oily, firm, white and some darker flesh; delicate flavour, larger kingfish have stronger flavour
leatherjacket	file fish, ocean jacket, cream fish	firm, white flesh, few bones; mild flavour
ling	pink ling	firm, moist, white flesh, large flakes; mild flavour
luderick	black fish, black bream	firm, oily flesh, few bones; distinctive flavour
mackerel, spanish	spotted mackerel, blue mackerel	firm, oily, white and some darker flesh; strong, distinctive flavour
mahi mahi	dolphinfish, dorado	firm, moist, white flesh; mild flavour
mirror dory	silver dory	firm, fine, moist flesh (similar to John dory, without the spot); sweet flavour
monkfish	anglerfish, stargazer	firm, moist, dense, white flesh; mild flavour
morwong	sea bream, rubberlip morwong, jackass fish, silver perch	fine, firm, white flesh, bony; mild flavour

SOLD AS	FRY	BAKE	POACH/STEAM	GRILL/BBQ	OTHER METHODS
fillets, fresh or preserved	yes	yes		yes	
whole, fillets, cutlets, smoked	yes	yes	yes	yes	raw (sashimi)
fillets		yes	yes		
whole, fillets, cutlets	yes	yes	yes	yes	
fillets, cutlets	yes	yes	yes	yes	
whole, fillets	yes	yes		yes	
steaks, cutlets	yes	yes		yes	
whole, fillets	yes	yes	yes	yes	
whole, fillets	yes	yes	yes	yes	
whole, fillets	yes	yes	yes	yes	
whole, fillets	yes	yes	yes	yes	
whole, fillets	yes	yes	yes	yes	
whole, fillets	yes	yes	yes	yes	
whole, fillets	yes	yes	yes	yes	
whole	yes	yes	yes	yes	
whole, fillets, cutlets, smoked	yes	yes	yes	yes	
fillets	yes	yes	yes	yes	
fillets	yes		yes		
whole	yes	yes		yes	
fillets	yes	yes	yes	yes	
whole, fillets	yes	yes	yes	yes	
whole, fillets, cutlets	yes	yes	yes	yes	raw (sashimi)
whole, fillets	yes	yes	yes	yes	
fillets	yes	yes	yes	yes	
whole, fillets	yes	yes	yes	yes	
whole, fillets, cutlets	yes	yes		yes	
fillets	yes	yes	yes	yes	
whole, fillets	yes	yes	yes	yes	
fillets	yes	yes		yes	
whole, fillets	yes	yes	yes		

SPECIES	ALSO KNOWN AS	CHARACTERISTICS
mullet, red	goatfish, barbounia, rouget	firm, white flesh; delicate flavour
mullet, sea	grey mullet, bully mullet	fine, oily, pink flesh; strong flavour
orange roughy	red roughy, sea perch, deep-sea perch	firm, white flesh, boneless; mild flavour
parrot fish	tuskfish	soft, white flesh; delicate flavour
perch, ocean	coral perch, rock cod	fine, white flesh, bony; delicate flavour
pike	shortfin pike, sea pike	firm, white flesh; sweet flavour
pilchard		oily, soft, dark flesh; distinctive flavour
red emperor		firm, moist, white flesh; delicate, sweet flavour
redfish	nannygai, red snapper	firm, white to pinkish flesh, bony; mild flavour
ribbonfish		soft, white flesh; delicate flavour
sardine	bluebait pilchards (adult)	soft, fine, oily flesh; strong flavour
shark	hake, flake	firm, moist, pink flesh, boneless; mild flavour
skate	ray	soft, white to pinkish flesh made up of cartilage; sweet, delicious flavour
snapper	cockney bream, red bream	firm, moist, slightly oily, white flesh, medium flakes; mild flavour
snook		soft, white to dark flesh; distinctive flavour
swordfish		firm, meaty flesh; mild flavour
tailor	skipjack	soft, slightly oily, pink flesh; distinctive flavour
trevally	silver or white trevally	firm, slightly oily, pink flesh; mild flavour
trout, coral	leopard, blue spot trout	firm, moist, white flesh; mild flavour
trout, ocean		firm, moist, delicate, orangy-pink flesh; sweet flavour
trout, rainbow	river trout, steel-head trout	soft, oily, pink flesh; mild, delicate, sometimes muddy flavour
trumpeter		moist, cream to pinkish flesh, medium flake; mild flavour
tuna, bluefin	southern bluefin	firm, oily (but dry when cooked) flesh, large flakes; distinctive flavour
tuna, yellowfin		firm, oily, deep-red flesh, large flakes; medium flavour
warehou, blue	snotty-nose trevalla, black trevalla, snotgall trevally	firm, slightly oily, white flesh; mild flavour
whitebait		tiny fish, eaten whole; delicate flavour
whiting, King George	spotted whiting	soft, white flesh; delicate, sweet flavour
whiting, sand	silver whiting	delicate, fine flesh, bony; delicate flavour
whiting, school	red spot whiting	fine, white flesh, bony; distinctive flavour

SOLD AS	FRY	BAKE	POACH/STEAM	GRILL/BBQ	OTHER METHODS
whole, fillets	yes	yes	yes	yes	
whole, fillets	yes	yes		yes	
fillets	yes	yes	yes	yes	
whole	yes	yes	yes	yes	
whole, fillets	yes	yes	yes	yes	deep-fry
whole	yes	yes	yes	yes	
whole, canned	yes	yes		yes	
whole, fillets, cutlets	yes	yes	yes	yes	
whole, fillets	yes	yes	yes	yes	
cutlets	yes	yes		yes	
whole, fillets, butterflied	yes	yes		yes	
fillets	yes	yes	yes	yes	
wings	yes	yes	yes	yes	
whole, fillets	yes	yes	yes	yes	raw (sashimi), smoke
cutlets	yes	yes		yes	
steaks	yes	yes		yes	smoke
whole	yes	yes		yes	
whole, fillets	yes	yes	yes	yes	
whole, fillets	yes	yes	yes	yes	
whole, cutlets, fillets	yes	yes	yes	yes	
whole, fresh and smoked	yes	yes		yes	
whole, fillets	yes	yes	yes	yes	
whole, steaks	yes	yes		yes	raw (sashimi)
steaks	yes	yes		yes	raw (sashimi)
fillets	yes	yes	yes	yes	smoke
whole	yes	yes			deep-fry
whole, fillets	yes	yes	yes	yes	
whole, fillets	yes	yes	yes	yes	
whole	yes	yes		yes	

107

SPECIES	ALSO KNOWN AS	CHARACTERISTICS
abalone (mollusc)	paua, earfish, muttonfish, ormer	large, ear-shaped, colourful shell; strong flavour
Balmain bugs (crustacean)	shovel-nosed lobster	orange-red when raw; mild, sweet flesh
blue swimmer crab (crustacean)	blue manner sand crab	moist, white flesh, shells bright blue, purple and white; delicate, sweet flavour
cockles (mollusc)	arkshell	grey, brown, pink or dark blue circular shell; distinctive flavour
cuttlefish (cephalopods)		white flesh, has an internal bone (cuttle bone or quill), oval body with tentacle; ink can be used in sauces or for colouring pasta; flavour similar to squid
lobster (crustacean)	crayfish, rock lobster, spiny lobster	ranges from yellow, orange, green, blue to almost black when raw; sweet, firm flesh (large flakes) in the tail and claws
marron (crustacean)	freshwater crayfish	range from brown to blue when raw; sweet, mild flavour
Moreton Bay bugs (crustacean)	bay lobster	orange-brown when raw; mild, sweet flavour
mud crab (crustacean)	mangrove crab	olive-green; rich, sweet flavour
mussels (mollusc)	black and green-lip mussel	dark blue, black and green; firm flesh; strong flavour
octopus (cephalopods)		soft flesh; mild, sweet flavour
oysters (mollusc)	common varieties: Sydney rock oyster, Pacific oyster	size varies according to species; plump, creamy flesh; distinctive flavour
pipis (mollusc)		small shells open like mussels when cooked; soak before use to remove sand; delicate, mild flavour
prawns (shrimp) (crustacean)	common varieties: school prawns, king prawns, banana prawns, tiger prawns, royal reds	raw prawns from creamy-yellow to pink, green, grey, olive-brown and blue; bright orange when cooked; round, plump meat with sweet flavour
scallops (mollusc)	commercial (Tasmanian), saucer (in shell)	commercial: white meat with orange roe attached, ridged fan-shaped shell; saucer: no roe, round, pink shell; sweet flavour
scampi (crustacean)	Dublin Bay prawn, langoustine, Norway lobster	similar to yabbie but much smaller claws, firm, moist flesh; sweet flavour
spanner crab (crustacean)	frog crab	orange, brittle shell when raw; sweet flavour
squid (cephalopod)	other varieties: calamari squid, arrow squid, ethridge squid	varies from mottled pink to grey when raw, turns white when cooked, tender if not over-cooked; calamari variety is the most tender; mild, sweet flavour
yabbie	freshwater crayfish	range from brown, green to purple; slightly muddy, sweet flavour

SOLD AS	FRY	BAKE	POACH/STEAM	GRILL/BBQ	OTHER METHODS
in shell or shucked	yes		yes		
live, cooked	yes	yes	yes	yes	boil
raw, cooked		yes	yes	yes	boil
in shell form only, live	yes	yes	yes	yes	
raw	yes	yes	yes	yes	deep-fry, stir-fry
live, cooked, tail available raw	yes	yes	yes	yes	boil
live, raw, cooked	yes		yes	yes	boil
live, cookod	yes	yes	yes	yes	boil
live		yes	yes		boil, stir-fry
live, shelled and cooked	yes	yes	yes	yes	boil, stir-fry
raw	yes		yes	yes	boil, stir-fry
raw, live in the shell; shelled and bottled	yes	yes	yes	yes	deep-fry, raw
live in shell	yes	yes	yes	yes	boil, stir-fry
raw, cooked, peeled, unpeeled	yes	yes	yes	yes	boil, stir-fry, deep-fry
raw and live in shell, freshly shucked in half shell, or shelled meat	yes	yes	yes	yes	deep-fry, stir-fry
live and raw	yes		yes	yes	
cooked		yes	yes		boil
raw, uncleaned or cleaned hoods (tubes), whole or cut into rings	yes	yes	yes	yes	deep-fry, stir-fry
live, raw, cooked	yes		yes	yes	boil

INDEX

From planning to publication, step-by-step recipe books are thoughtfully compiled to ensure the home cook can proceed with confidence and is delighted with the results every time.

■ Appropriate recipes are carefully selected and experienced recipe writers write and test their recipes
■ Every recipe goes through a rigid testing process in the step-by-step Test Kitchens
■ All recipes are tested and presented to a tasting panel for comment
■ All ingredients are easy to find in your local shops
■ Many cooking procedures are shown in our step-by-step photographs, which are carefully planned to boost the cook's confidence
■ Practical hints are provided to take the hard work out of cooking
■ To cater to today's informed consumer, all recipes include a thorough nutritional breakdown

INTERNATIONAL GLOSSARY OF INGREDIENTS

capsicum	red or green pepper	English spinach	spinach
Chinese beans	snake beans	snow peas	mange tout
fresh coriander	fresh cilantro	tomato purée (Aus.)	tomato purée, double
courgette	zucchini		concentrate (UK)
eggplant	aubergine		

This edition published in 2006 by Bay Books, an imprint of Murdoch Books Pty Limited, Pier 8/9, 23 Hickson Road, Millers Point, NSW 2000, Australia.

Managing Editor: Rachel Carter **Editor:** Wendy Stephen **Designer:** Wing Ping Tong **Food Director:** Jody Vassallo **Managing Food Editor:** Jane Lawson **Food Editor:** Rebecca Clancy **Recipe Development:** Julie Ballard, Rebecca Clancy, Jenny Fanshaw, Fiona Hammond, Barbara Lowery, Kate Murdoch, Maria Papadopalous, Sally Parker, Margot Smithyman, Wendy Quisumbing, Jody Vassallo **Home Economists:** Alison Adams, Julie Ballard, Kate Murdoch, Justine Poole, Wendy Quisumbing, Michelle Thrift **Nutritionist:** Susanna Holt **Photographers:** Craig Cranko, Reg Morrison (steps) **Food Stylist:** Sarah de Nardi **Food Preparation:** Justine Poole

Chief Executive: Juliet Rogers **Publisher:** Kay Scarlett

ISBN 1-74045-935-0
Printed by Sing Cheong Printing Co. Ltd. Printed in China.